Praise for *The 3 Secrets to Effective Time Investment*

As Elizabeth lovingly but pressingly reminds us, "You can't give to others what you don't have"—particularly when it comes to time. She eloquently moves us past traditional and outdated concepts around time *management* and instead lays a compelling foundation for time *investment*—so that we can all focus on what matters most to our individual lives and careers. This book is clear, compelling, and action-oriented, with a brilliant mix of stories, principles, reflection questions, and action steps to help you move past your blocks, invest your time wisely, and ultimately transform your life in the process.

—JENNY BLAKE, AUTHOR OF *LIFE AFTER COLLEGE: THE COMPLETE GUIDE TO GETTING WHAT YOU WANT*

This is much more than a "time management" book. Elizabeth possesses deeply meaningful expertise in helping others to design the fulfilling, peaceful lifestyles of their dreams—and she shares it *all* in this incredible resource. Whether you simply need help fine-tuning your schedule, or you're ready to make massive shifts that will catapult you to places your soul has always longed to go, you'll get there with the ingeniously personalized systems, tools, and advice in this book.

—AMANDA AITKEN, FOUNDER AND CEO, THE GIRL'S GUIDE TO WEB DESIGN AND BETTER THAN CHOCOLATE WEB & BRANDING

This book is magical. To achieve your dreams, you need to define actions allowing you to invest in your priorities. Elizabeth helps you do that and also to strengthen the routines that make these actions automatic.

—ASH KUMRA, DREAMITALIVE.COM COFOUNDER, "CONFESSIONS FROM AN ENTREPRENEUR" SERIES AUTHOR AND PUBLIC SPEAKER

If you struggle with using your time efficiently, then you have to read this book. Elizabeth provides fantastic tips about how you can stay on top of things without being stressed out.

—HASSAN OSMAN, PMP—SENIOR MANAGER AT CISCO SYSTEMS
AND BLOGGER AT WWW.THECOUCHMANAGER.COM

If you are going to go from ordinary to extraordinary success, you need to invest your time in your top priorities. Elizabeth teaches you how to do just that and to make it as easy as possible through simple routines.

—SCOTT GERBER, FOUNDER OF THE YOUNG ENTERPRISE COUNCIL

THE 3 SECRETS
TO EFFECTIVE
TIME INVESTMENT

*How to Achieve More Success
with Less Stress*

ELIZABETH GRACE SAUNDERS

New York Chicago San Francisco Lisbon London
Madrid Mexico City Milan New Delhi
San Juan Seoul Singapore
Sydney Toronto

1 2 3 4 5 6 7 8 9 0   DOC/DOC   1 8 7 6 5 4 3 2

ISBN   978-0-07-180881-1
MHID   0-07-180881-7

e-ISBN   978-0-07-180882-8
e-MHID   0-07-180882-5

McGraw-Hill books are available at special quantity discounts to use as premiums and
sales promotions or for use in corporate training programs. To contact a representative,
please e-mail us at bulksales@mcgraw-hill.com.

This book is printed on acid-free paper.

*Dedicated to all those who hope for change
and are willing to pursue peace,*

*And to the dream of a world full of people who
feel peaceful, confident, accomplished, known,
and loved because they invest their time wisely.*

CONTENTS

To best explain my enthusiasm for Elizabeth Grace Saunders and her provocative ideas about life management, I need to rewind the clock to the year leading up to our first meeting. At the time, I was a graduate student at MIT. I had, by that point, published a pair of advice guides for college students.

My academic strategies worked well. I knew this because I had painstakingly researched them and had a growing collection of case studies to support their effectiveness. College, it turns out, is not as hard as students would like us and, more important, their parents to believe. Even relatively simple habits can spark big improvements. Consider, for example, the concept of a Sunday ritual. This strategy requires you to sit down with your calendar on Sunday night and plan your week ahead: Figure out what is due, what work needs to be done, and when you're going to do the work. To adult ears, this sounds absurdly straightforward, but to the typical overwhelmed student, it can be life-changing.

My books teemed with stories of relaxed Rhodes Scholars and valedictorians who finish studying by dinner. The growing student stress problem, I argued, was due to lack of information. Students struggle because no one taught them how to be good students. If you gave me a few hours to explain better strategies, I believed I could transform *any* student into a high-scoring, low-stress star. Because I had just launched a blog, I decided to use it to publically prove my point. I announced that I would take on a group of overwhelmed undergraduates, transform them into model students, and post about the whole process.

It was this decision that led me to Leena (Leena's name was changed to preserve her anonymity)—which is where my story veers off the expected path and puts me on a collision course with Elizabeth and her ideas.

I began working with Leena in the fall of 2007. At the time, she was a soph-omore at MIT who was overwhelmed with obligations, underwhelmed with her grades, and not getting much sleep. We met in the common area outside my office in MIT's Stata Center. I had her walk me through her commitments and list her issues. After hearing her summary, I took a blank sheet of paper and drew a weekly calendar that split up each day into hours. I began by adding her classes, her labs, and optimistic estimates of the time required to tackle homework. I then started adding time for her extracurricular commitments. At some point during this process, the schedule filled from early in the morning until late at night, seven days a week, with almost no breaks.

"Even if you're 100 percent organized and use my best, most efficient study strategies," I told her, pointing out the obvious, "you literally don't have enough hours in the day for your current load." I then gave her my prescription: She needed to significantly reduce her academic and extra-curricular obligations and then tackle what remained with an upgraded set of fine-tuned habits. This would provide her with enough time to actually stand out in her courses and activities and would eliminate her feeling of constant overwhelm.

To me, the plan was a no-brainer. Leena disagreed. She politely thanked me for my advice and even came to several follow-up meetings. But she ignored my recommendations, leaving her load untouched and holding out hope that some magic productivity strategy could make it all work. After another rough semester, she ended up taking time off from MIT for medical leave. Leena's schedule had finally led to burnout, culminating with her failing to hand in a take-home final examination, even after sev-eral extensions. She returned home to the West Coast to rest and recover.

It was around this time that a common friend introduced me to Elizabeth and her work. At a high level, Elizabeth's work as a time coach for profes-sional clients was similar to my work with students: We both helped peo-ple take control of their life and lead it somewhere better. But Elizabeth's approach was different from my own. My instinct was to jump straight

into small-scale strategies. I assumed people knew what they *should* be doing; they just needed help doing it more efficiently. Elizabeth knew better. Her process started not with the details of her clients' current schedule, but the big-picture questions about what they really wanted to spend their time on. A big part of this effort was tackling negative beliefs and fears. She realized, for example, that learning how to confidently say "No" could be more important than how you handle the requests you accept. It was only after achieving this clarity that she would transition her clients toward the small-scale strategies of daily time management.

This insight is exactly what I lacked when dealing with Leena. Though I didn't know it at the time, Leena craved the type of values-driven process Elizabeth pioneered. She was confused about what was she was trying to accomplish at college. Later, she admitted to me that her overstuffed scheduled was driven by her fear that she would "miss out" on some unidentified calling. She was also fearful that she was an imposter—a common worry at elite schools—which led her to equate stress with validation that she was earning her keep. When I blithely told Leena to drastically reduce her obligations, to her mind, this translated as a request to give up on success and admit that she didn't belong at MIT.

No wonder she ignored me.

It was soon after the Leena disaster that Elizabeth helped expose me to the psychological/emotional side of life management. This exposure changed my worldview. In 2008, I turned the focus of my blog from describing study strategies to tackling the deeper issues surrounding student stress. I introduced the "Zen valedictorian" philosophy, which argued that the goal for school should be to achieve success *and* happiness, and then I wrote article after article convincing students to embrace this mind-set. I even went on to write a book that applied the Zen valedictorian philosophy to high school, showing students how to navigate the college admissions gauntlet without suffering overload. The response to my new focus was overwhelming. Whereas I used to receive polite notes from students thanking me for helping them become more organized, I now started to receive effusive messages from students thanking me for transforming their lives. I appreciated the kind words but couldn't help but feel that these notes should have been cc'd to Elizabeth, whose ideas helped to make these transformations possible.

....

The book you're holding is not just another collection of tips for organizing your schedule. It's a guide to overhauling your life—a guide based on years of practical coaching experience and backed by science. Elizabeth has helped countless people figure out what matters and then shown them how to transform these priorities from slogans into action. This book reveals the details of this system for the first time. Given the success I've had applying her philosophy in my own work, you can understand my excitement that she's finally sharing these ideas with the rest of the world.

Early in the book, Elizabeth emphasizes, "You have a choice to be different starting now." I encourage you to embrace this opportunity. The concrete, tested steps in the pages ahead will take you from the big picture to the small and leave you with a life that is peaceful and successful, a state that Elizabeth aptly describes as "work-life brilliance." I've experienced this state many times close up, and I can tell you, without reservation, that it's absolutely worth pursuing. So read on. . . .

Calvin Newport
August 15, 2012
Georgetown University
Washington, DC

Welcome to the adventure of effective time investment, and congratulations on taking the first step by opening up this book! Within these pages, you will discover three secrets for achieving more success with less stress. Here are three potential routes for your journey:

- **Read this front to back.** If you feel overwhelmed and uncertain of where to begin, read this book in full. This book starts by providing a guiding light through the dark, often unexplored areas of why people struggle with effective time investment. After laying the foundation, it then reveals the three secrets and how to implement them.
- **Focus on the most needed parts.** If you are fairly solid in your basic time investment skills but have some weak spots or areas you desire to refine, jump to the sections where you want the most help. The table of contents will show you how to zoom in on what matters to you.
- **Skip to the done-for-you routines.** If you just want an initial quick fix on a topic such as exercising or e-mail, head to the quick reference section. These done-for-you routines give you a starting point that you can then use "as is" or customize to fit your personality and lifestyle.

A Few Notes

- Think of this as a process where you celebrate consistently (not necessarily constantly) achieving more success with less stress.
- If you choose route two or three and find that you're not taking off, circle back and read the entire book. If you try to implement tactics without first confronting underlying issues, you are trying to fly a shiny shell of a plane without a strong engine.

- If you want all the latest and greatest time investment tips, go to www.ScheduleMakeover.com.

  Now, it's time to begin!
  To your brilliance!

  Elizabeth

A journey of a thousand miles begins with a single step.

—LAO TZU

THE FOUNDATION

CHAPTER 1

EFFECTIVE TIME INVESTMENT

Achieve More Success with Less Stress

It isn't what you have, or who you are, or where you are,
or what you are doing that makes you happy or unhappy.
It is what you think about.

—DALE CARNEGIE

The Seductress

It all began innocently enough at the end of a hectic day.

In an attempt to loosen some of the tension in your shoulders, rest your eyes, and regain the ability to focus, you had leaned back in your chair, putting your torso at an obtuse angle with your work surface and allowing your feet to splay out a bit in front of you.

You squeezed your eyes shut and then stretched them wide open a few times. Blink. Blink. Blink. You rolled around your neck. Crickle. Crack. And you extended your fingers out and then clenched them into tight fists. Out. In. As if this action could get your internal pistons firing enough to squeeze the last bit of productivity out of a day that had already left you dry—or, more accurately, parched.

But then you somewhat abruptly sat up, your body at attention and alert. Someone . . . or something . . . had delicately brushed a fingertip along your shoulder.

"Crazy!" you thought. "I'm the only one here. But yet I'm sure I felt something."

Cautiously, you swiveled your head like a submarine periscope looking for danger.

You don't see anyone, but you do hear a whisper in your ear. "You know," she begins in a low, poignant tone, "if you stay late tonight, we could get soooooooooo much done."

"But that's ridiculous!" you retort. "I've already done too much today. I need to get my mind off work and take a break for a while."

"But what about tomorrow?" she continues undeterred. "You'll have so much to do if you leave. If you stay with me now—where we're alone and it's quiet—you'll feel so good in the morning. You'll do what needs to be done. You'll be in control, in charge, and just about everyone will think you're amazing."

"Really?" you ask, a bit incredulously but starting to warm up to the idea.

"Really," she echoes back to you with a slight edge of triumph in her voice.

Your brow furrows as you ponder whether you should accept this advance from the initially unwelcome but increasingly attractive stranger. On the one hand, you feel exhausted, and you just want to exhale and truly kick back. On the other hand, though, you think that maybe she has a point, and you begin to doubt your initial intentions. Maybe I'm just lazy. Maybe staying later would really help me to dig out from this never-ending backlog. Maybe it will only be for one night.

So you stay that evening and do get a bit more done than usual.

But it soon becomes clear that your visitor desires more than a one-night stand; she wants you one night, then two, and then three.

What initially began as a reluctant decision on your part becomes an obsessive passion. You know you can't sustain the pace. You know that you risk losing all you hold dear—your relationships, your interests, your health, yourself.

Yet you no longer know how to resist the siren song of the Seductress of Overwork.

The Couch Potato

He came in *completely* uninvited.

No doorbell ring. No knock. No nothing.

He just meandered in as if he owned the place, plopped down on the couch, and started to blankly flip through TV channels.

"How absolutely bizarre," you thought to yourself as you happened to catch the back of his head, complete with a shock of unkempt hair, on your way to the kitchen to grab a glass of water. "I didn't expect a visitor."

But he seemed harmless, and you thought maybe someone else gave him permission to pass a bit of time in the living room, so you shook your head and then went back to your computer.

A few days passed without disturbance. Then he came back.

Longer this time—and the next and the next.

Soon it seemed as if this strange man, who had an unquenchable thirst for endless streams of TV programming and a voracious appetite for all things sweet, salty, and generally within the category of nonnutritious (the escalating grocery bills astounded you!), had taken up permanent residence in your home.

He never said a word or even really made eye contact with you.

But his presence shifted the energy of the house: gradually . . . subtly . . . a sense of general malaise descended like a dense, dank fog over an environment that once quivered with vibrant, focused productivity.

You no longer sprang out of bed in the morning, but instead you hit "Snooze" until your alarm got tired. Then—eventually—you rolled off the edge of your bed in an attempt to plunge yourself into the cold reality of the day.

But somehow even once you got vertical, everything seemed difficult. He was always there, and his nonverbal communication said it all: Why are you working so hard? Will it really come to anything? Why not just sit down next to me for a second . . . or two? It's so much easier not to do anything. Why don't you just treat yourself? Give yourself a break. Kick back and relax a little. You can always do that work tomorrow . . . or the next day. Just one more show. Do you want another drink? How about a donut? I've only eaten half the box. . . .

Before you knew it, the *entire* day slipped away like a glistening rivulet of water circling and then slipping down a drain.

What did you have to show for it? Nothing.

"Errrrrrr. . . . This is *so* frustrating," you think to yourself, letting out a grunt of angry disgust. "I need to do more. I must do better next time. I will set my alarm earlier. I will get up and do everything all at once."

But once the Couch Potato of Ambivalence took up residence, the strong opposing forces of desiring to achieve high productivity and wanting to simply relax and do nothing resulted in a listless, emotionless, seemingly insurmountable state of dullness.

Your Choice

Do either of these scenarios sound familiar? Or maybe both, depending on the situation? (Just for the record: The Seductress can show up at home, and the Couch Potato has been known to become a squatter in the most formal of offices.) If so, I can reassure you that you're not alone. As the founder and CEO of Real Life E Time Coaching & Training, I've built a business around helping people in these situations take back control of their time and their life.[1]

It's often not your fault that you find yourself trapped in a vicious cycle. Usually the onset happens so slowly and subtly that you don't realize what's happened until you have a seemingly unchangeable compulsion to act in a certain way.

Given the right environment, almost everyone has the potential to succumb to the Seductress of Overwork or the Couch Potato of Ambivalence. You shouldn't feel guilty or ashamed of being tempted, or even for times when you haven't made the best time investment choices. You can't change the past. But you can learn from it and . . .

This is *huge*, so really focus in here: *You have a choice to be different starting now.*

You can take the principles in this book and apply them to your life in a way that works best for you. Or you can give up and go back to the status quo.

Which path will you choose?

If you decide that enough is enough and you're ready for action, I would like you to flip to Chapter 7, pick one routine that you will begin implementing today, and then come back to this spot. The energy you

receive from this immediate positive behavioral change will help to give you the momentum to keep at this process of learning how to invest your time effectively.

Why Time Investment?

I am about to share with you three truths so profound, so earth-shattering, *so true* that they might make you fall over. If you're standing up, I suggest that you grab a chair. Are you seated? Good.

Time Truth #1: Time Is Limited

Let's end the debate about whether you can have it all, do it all, or be it all. We'll talk about work-life brilliance in the next section and your personal definition of success in Chapter 4. But the bottom-line, undeniable truth is that everyone—rich or poor, young or old, male or female—has 24 hours in a day and seven days in a week. No more and no less.

The difference in whether people achieve more success with less stress comes down to how they choose to invest that time. Since time is a finite resource, by definition, using more of it for one activity decreases the amount that you have for another. For instance, if you spend 10 hours of your day at work, 7 hours sleeping, and 2 hours commuting, you have exactly 5 hours left to fit in everything else from brushing your teeth to talking to your family to reading a book. Increases in the time allocation in any of these areas will further reduce your open time.

The solution for how you can live in alignment with this time truth is to practice Secret #1: Clarify Action-Based Priorities.

Time Truth #2: Reality Always Wins

Do you regularly stop to think through the reality of exactly how much time you have to spend? Do you count the cost when you either succumb to the Seductress of Overwork and give more than the proper share to production or when you sink in beside the Coach Potato of Ambivalence and fritter away the hours?

In my experience helping people around the world to organize their time, most people don't. This is a big part of why I'm writing this book. I want to get people away from the mentality of frantically trying to "manage time," which often leads to the scheduling equivalent of smashing more papers into an already overflowing file drawer. We instead want to think strategically about the portfolio of our lives, investing only in our top priorities and making sure that we have the proper allocation of resources. The plain fact is this: Sixty hours of work will never fit into 40 hours of time, and activities that have no time budgeted for them will not happen. As famed investor and philanthropist Warren Buffett wisely stated, "The rich invest in time; the poor invest in money."

You can embrace this time truth by following Secret #2: Set Realistic Expectations.

Time Truth #3: Habit Patterns Rule

At our very best, we may choose to do something that we find difficult because it's our priority. But usually we're not at our very best. We're tired, hungry, angry, lonely, bored, stressed, or any other number of things that make doing the right thing extremely difficult. Our willpower is limited, so, in general, our actions will follow the path of least resistance. Like water running down a mountain riverbed or electricity coursing through wires, our habit patterns determine where we automatically invest most of our time.

With the increased intensity of the fight against distraction caused by the nonstop inundation of technology, you must increase the strength of your tactics against the enemy. As Aristotle said, "You are what you repeatedly do." The essential truth in all of this is that you will invest your time as you have trained yourself to invest it through consistent repetition.

The way to leverage this time truth is to drill in Secret #3: Strengthen Simple Routines.

We live in a totally wired world where everyone from our boss to our Facebook friend and everything from our phone to our TV attempt to grab our attention. With the loss of natural boundaries, we need to vigilantly and intentionally decide how to invest our time; otherwise, it will be spent

for us. Following these three secrets to effective time investment leads to the achievement of what I like to call *work-life brilliance.*

The Work-Life Brilliance Solution

Now that you are starting to see how effective time investment can help you to address some fundamental time truths, it's time to talk about the end goal. I call this *work-life brilliance.* The exact details of work-life brilliance (in terms of time allocation and corresponding routines) vary depending on your unique situation (such as your priorities or energy levels), but the concept remains the same.

What Work-Life Brilliance Is Not About

- Trying to force you into a rigid, one-size-fits-all set of rules removed from the reality of the dynamic nature of life.
- Judging your priorities. (You decide what's important to you, and this book helps you to figure out how to invest your time as you see best.)
- Making you feel incompetent or giving you a license to judge, criticize, or blame others. (If you struggle with pointing fingers, make sure to read the section in Chapter 9 entitled, "What Frustrates Planners about Spontaneous People and Vice Versa.")

What Work-Life Brilliance Is About

- Developing a system of time investment that allows you to achieve more success with less stress
- Practicing these three time investment secrets: clarify action-based priorities, set realistic expectations, and strengthen simple routines
- Affirming your right to choose—and feel good about—what you do and what you don't do, and aligning your thoughts, emotions, and actions
- Recovering quickly after a setback, such as getting sick, and responding with agility to an unexpected schedule change
- Practicing intentional routines that make directing your time investment toward your personal definition of success the path of least

resistance (Find a step-by-step guide to defining success your way in Chapter 4.)

Life is messy, not perfect. That's okay. It takes dirtying the kitchen to create a lavish feast. But you can enjoy the journey and achieve work-life brilliance through the strategies in the coming chapters. This will benefit not only you but also everyone around you. When you have better organizational strategies, you can perform better in all your roles as a business owner, an employee, a coworker, a boss, a freelancer, a dad, a mom, a significant other, a wife, a husband, a sister, a brother, a friend, a neighbor, or any of the other ways that you relate to others. Not only will you be so much nicer to be around, but you'll also have more to give to those who matter most to you.

- You can't give others what you don't have—whether it's something tangible like money or intangible like time.
- You can't authentically teach people what you don't know.

> WARNING: When you start practicing these principles, you risk inspiring, encouraging, and teaching all those around you how they too can experience work-life brilliance, or perhaps school-life brilliance! It's somewhat contagious.

This journey won't be easy (it's a bit like muscle training for your brain), but by practicing the three secrets in this book, you can build your capacity to achieve more success with less stress.

Here are some example schedules to illustrate how work-life brilliance and effective time investment can look different for individuals with varying circumstances and priorities (see Figures 1.1 to 1.3).

The Impact of Your Time Investment Choices

The way you decide to invest your time can have a dramatic life-or-death impact. A University College London professor, Mika Kivimaki, did a 12-year research study of more than 7,000 people. Of this group, only 10 percent worked more than 11 hours per day. However, those who pulled long hours had 67 percent of the heart attacks of the entire study.[2]

Hour	Monday	Tuesday	Wednesday	Thursday	Friday	Saturday	Sunday
7:00	Rise and shine, coffee						
7:30	Get ready, breakfast, and children to school						
8:00							
8:30	To-do list and e-mail						
9:00						Saturday morning breakfast	
9:30	Business activities						
10:00							
10:30							Church
11:00							
11:30							
Noon	Lunch and exercise						
12:30							
1:00	Business activities						
1:30							
2:00							
2:30	Wrap-up and final e-mail check					Coffee meeting for business	
3:00	Children home from school: Snack, homework, and housework						
3:30							
4:00							
4:30	Go to the park or play with the neighbors						
5:00							
5:30	Dinner prep while children take baths						
6:00	Dinner and cleanup					Evening out with friends	Weekly planning, meal planning, and grocery shopping
6:30							
7:00	Final homework, reading, and housework						
7:30							
8:00	Children to bed						
8:30	Connect with spouse						
9:00							
9:30	Read, pray, and meditate						
10:00	Sleep						

FIGURE 1.1 *Parent building a business while the children are in school.*

Hour	Monday	Tuesday	Wednesday	Thursday	Friday	Saturday	Sunday
5:00	Arise and meditation						
5:30	Work on important project						
6:00							
6:30							
7:00	Breakfast, shower, and commute into the office						
7:30							
8:00	Answer e-mail and daily planning						
8:30							
9:00	Meetings, project work, and strategic work					Clean up house	
9:30							
10:00						Call parents	
10:30							
11:00						Work project	
11:30							
Noon	E-mail						
12:30							
1:00	Lunch with a mentor, coworker, or networking connection						
1:30							
2:00	Project work	Meetings, project work, or strategic work			Strategic work		Go sailing
2:30							
3:00						Play soccer	
3:30							
4:00							
4:30							
5:00							
5:30	Wrap up and evaluate the day						
6:00	Commute home, mentally decompress						
6:30							
7:00	Exercise	Drinks with friends	Exercise	Favorite TV show	Out with friends directly after work	BBQ with neighbors	
7:30							
8:00							
8:30	Dinner						
9:00	E-mail or project wrap-up						Weekly planning
9:30							
10:00	Read						
10:30	Sleep						Sleep

FIGURE 1.2 *Executive focused on career advancement.*

Hour	Monday	Tuesday	Wednesday	Thursday	Friday	Saturday	Sunday
6:00	Wake up and walk the dog						
6:30							
7:00	Eat breakfast and get ready						
7:30	Listen to relaxing music on the commute to work						
8:00	Weekly planning	Meetings and administrative work				Do school projects at the library	
8:30							
9:00							
9:30	Meetings and administrative work						
10:00							
10:30							
11:00	E-mail						
11:30							
Noon	Lunch with colleagues						
12:30	Project work						
1:00							
1:30							
2:00						Go biking or to the gym	
2:30							
3:00						Longer walk with the dog	
3:30							
4:00	Wrap-up, final e-mail check, and planning for the next day						
4:30							
5:00	Commute home, dinner, take dog out, and walk dog if no evening class						
5:30							
6:00	Exercise	In class at university			Social activities with friends		Finish school work if not completed
6:30							
7:00	Laundry, grocery, and housework						
7:30							
8:00							
8:30							
9:00		Exercise					
9:30							
10:00							
10:30	Read, meditate, and do something else refreshing						
11:00	Sleep						

FIGURE 1.3 *Full-time employee by day and student by night.*

Even if you don't foresee an early demise by overwork, you should know that I've heard numerous successful people say that effective time investment is the single most important factor in releasing their potential and experiencing the life they desire.

With this in mind, it's time for you to start actively engaging with this material. Under each of the following sections, I've included a space for you to write down the results you've seen from your current time investment choices.

Yes, writing in this book will lower its resale value on Amazon (but you're going to treasure it forever, right?), but admitting in an external way what's happening has a huge impact on your motivation to put in the hard work it takes to keep doing what's working and to change what's not. If you're enjoying this book on an e-reader, you can go to www.reallifee .com/tib to download and print the worksheet entitled, "The Impact of Your Time Investment Choices," to help you complete this exercise.

When the Seductress or the Couch Potato try to weasel their way back into your life, return to your answers in this section to remind yourself why you have no time for them.

To Complete This Exercise

1. Rate your time investment choices in these areas on a scale of 1 to 10, with a perfect 10 meaning that you invest your time exactly as you desire in this area and a 1 meaning that your time investment is dramatically misaligned with your priorities.
2. List the specific ways your time investment choices in these areas have had an impact on you. This will start to give you a clearer sense of exactly what actions you may want to increase or decrease in your life and give you motivation to change.

Physically

How have your time investment choices had an impact on you physically? Consider: blood pressure, sleep, exercise, eating, energy levels, and weight.

Current rating:

▶ **RED FLAGS:** You know or others tell you that you need to make some changes for the sake of your physical health. You feel tired, sluggish, and tense most of the time.

Mentally

How have your time investment choices had an impact on you mentally? Consider: focus, problem-solving ability, strategic thinking, learning, and information retention.

Current rating:

> ▶ **RED FLAGS:** You forget things, have trouble making decisions, can't figure out where to focus, don't know what to do when, and have a mental "dullness."

Emotionally

How have your time investment choices had an impact on you emotionally? Consider: self-control, empathy, patience, response to problems, graciousness, spontaneous tears, and yelling.

Current rating:

> ▶ **RED FLAGS:** You respond harshly, feel like you can't handle many things, feel overwhelmed by challenges, act impatiently, and have little capacity to "deal with" other people's emotions.

Spiritually

How have your time investment choices had an impact on you spiritually? Consider: sense of connectedness, feeling peaceful, prayer, meditation, spiritual reading, and group attendance.

Current rating:

> ▶ **RED FLAGS:** You feel uncentered, disconnected, restless, purposeless, anxious, and like you aren't doing what you were meant to do in life.

Relationally

How have your time investment choices had an impact on you relationally? Consider: boss, colleagues, clients, employees, subcontractors, family, friends, significant other, professional network, neighbors, and strangers.

Current rating:

> ▶ **RED FLAGS:** You sense a lack of communication, fulfillment, and connection in key relationships. You feel like you're being nagged or having to nag others, and you ignore or snap at people when they unexpectedly come across your path or inconvenience you in some way.

Productivity

How have your time investment choices had an impact on your productivity? Consider: getting what's most important done, moving forward on big projects, keeping up on regular processing, and feeling confident that you know what's most important and that you're doing it.

Current rating:

> ▶ **RED FLAGS:** You seem very busy, yet you feel like you get very few important activities done. You fail to make progress on your biggest projects. You tend to wander through the day instead of approaching it in a focused manner.

Great work on completing the questionnaire! Now it's time to do a bit of self-reflection. Did anything surprise you as you did this exercise? Where do you think your results look pretty strong, that is, more positive than negative? Where do they come up lacking, that is, you noticed some of the red flags or low ratings?

In the coming chapters we'll talk through how you can make completely different time investment choices or slightly enhance the ones that work fairly well for you already. But this exercise needed to come first so that you could know why it's worth the effort to rebuild your habits and to remind you of what's really most important for you to improve. It might be that exercising more or simply taking more time to rest will have a larger overall positive impact than a few extra minutes of professional productivity.

Remember: You will only get what you need to get out of the preceding exercise—and out of this entire book—when you are completely honest. This is a judgment-free zone. Where you start now matters much less than your choice to make consistent progress toward what you believe constitutes the best investment of your time in the future.

WHAT YOU WANT TO DO
VERSUS WHAT YOU LONG TO DO

Before we move on, let's take a moment to quickly address a mental battle that many people face: They believe that if they don't feel like doing something, that means that they don't *want* to do something and therefore can't do it.

But that's simply not the case.

What you feel like is what you *long* to do based on physical sensations (e.g., fatigue, panic attack, or muscle tension) or emotions (e.g., sadness, love, fear, or anger). What you *want* to do is what not only will fulfill you in the moment but also will serve your highest priorities. You can develop routines that help you to do what you really want to do even if you don't always feel like making the best choices in the moment.

As a very simple, tangible example of this truth, let's talk about healthy eating. Personally, I have a priority to stay at a healthy weight for my height. Therefore, I need to consistently eat nutritious foods. However, I love sweets and am a total carb fiend. (If I had to choose just one food to eat all the time, I would select fresh baked bread with a cinnamon swirl and a sugar crumble topping. My mouth has started watering simply by writing of this deliciousness.) What I feel like or *long* to do is to eat as many sweets as possible.

But what I really *want* to do is to eat healthy foods overall.

Given this knowledge, I exert a huge amount of self-discipline at the grocery store. I carefully think through anything unhealthy that I put into my cart, trying to limit it to one item per shopping trip, and then reassessing everything again before I check out to make sure that I'm aligning my food choices with what I really want. During the week, I decide how much I will eat of my most favorite pleasure foods. But I need to exert much less willpower and get good results because I don't have too many unhealthy options to pick from in my home.

Does this start to clarify the difference between *longing for* and *wanting* something?

You can use the same type of process for all sorts of areas where what you naturally long to do differs from what you want to do. The next section, on time personality, will help you to understand your natural propensities and how to embrace them in this process of change.

Your Time Personality

I am a huge fan of personality tests. I find that they offer invaluable insight into why we do what we do and also help us to understand other people's perspectives.

I wanted to touch briefly on three fundamental differences in *time personality* that will come up again in more detail later in this book. Having tendencies in one direction or the other isn't a sign of having a character flaw or being lazy, it's simply a fact. It's important for you to recognize your natural time personality and work with it, not against it, to experience lasting behavioral change.

- **Spontaneous versus planner.** In short, spontaneous types prefer to go with the flow. Planners prefer to know what they will do when. For more insight on these opposing perspectives, go to Chapter 9.
- **Moderator versus abstainer.** Moderators can do just a little bit of something, whereas abstainers tend to have a more all-or-nothing approach. When you design your custom routines in Chapter 7, you'll need to keep this in mind in order to have realistic expectations about what will be sustainable for you.
- **Embrace versus build.** If you prefer to embrace change, you do better when you add five new routines at once. If you prefer to build change, you're better off mastering one change before moving on to the next one. Keep these preferences in mind when you begin adding new routines to your life.

You can also experience changes in time personality based on whether or not you feel stressed. Take a quick moment to think through what important activities get neglected when you feel under pressure.

What You Just Brainstormed Can Help You in Two Ways

- When you notice yourself starting to exhibit behavior corresponding with your "stressed" self, you can take that as an early warning sign that something needs to change, and adapt accordingly.
- You'll want to define some important activities that tend to fall out of your schedule when you are under stress, such as spending time with friends, washing dishes, or having one-on-one meetings with direct reports. You can turn these items into routines such as monthly dinners, pre-bedtime tidying, or recurring touch-base meetings so that you consistently exhibit your best behavior even when you don't feel your best.

If you would like a more in-depth examination of what makes you tick, I also recommend looking at these tools:

- **Myers-Briggs Type Indicator (www.myersbriggs.org).** This test classifies four components of your personality so that you can get a better idea of how you perceive the world and make decisions. Looking at the descriptions of the judging versus perceiving component will help a great deal with understanding your time investment preferences.
- **Riso-Hudson Enneagram Type Indicator (www.enneagraminstitute .com).** This tool helps you not only to see your natural personality but also to determine how you tend to respond when under stress and how your personality can develop in a positive way as you progress emotionally and mentally.
- **StrengthsFinder (www.strengthsfinder.com).** This Gallup research–based assessment gives you a clear understanding of your strengths, how to leverage them, and how to get support from people with complementary strengths.

Also, if you struggle with any of the following symptoms, you may want to have a professional assessment for attention deficit disorder (ADD) or attention deficit hyperactivity disorder (ADHD):

- Trouble concentrating and staying focused or being hyperfocused, where you become so engrossed in activities that you neglect other things you want to do

- Disorganization, forgetfulness, hyperactivity, or restlessness
- Impulsivity and difficulty with emotional management

For Further Information on ADD and ADHD, Go To

- **Children and Adults with Attention Deficit/Hyperactivity Disorder (www.chadd.org).**
- **Attention Deficit Disorder Association (www.add.org).**
- **Self Help for Adult ADD/ADHD (www.helpguide.org/mental/adhd _add_adult_strategies.htm).**
- **National Institute of Mental Health (www.nimh.nih.gov/health/ topics/attention-deficit-hyperactivity-disorder-adhd/index.shtml).**

This leads us to the final section before we launch into the wild world of emotions—behavioral change, that is, why there's hope for you even if investing your time well has never come naturally.

Why There's Hope!

No matter where you start with your time investment skills, you can improve. For some people, activities such as planning the day or keeping a calendar come quite easily. For others, these skills seem excruciatingly difficult. But much like learning how to play a musical instrument or speak another language, your current skill level doesn't indicate your potential ability but rather serves as an initial benchmark.

In *9 Things Successful People Do Differently*,[3] Heidi Grant Halvorson explains how research reveals why you can change and what it takes:

> *Incremental theorists . . . believe that ability is malleable—that it can and does change with effort and experience. And according to the evidence, they are perfectly right. You can get more ability if you want more. All you need is grit.*
>
> *Grit, in the sense that psychologists use the term, is persistence and commitment to long-term goals.*

The good news: Change is possible. The bad news: It takes effort.

Depending on your starting point and your natural strengths, this could seem like a joy ride or like a marathon. But I can assure you that if you consistently struggle with time investment, the effort to get better is worth it. Successful people in all kinds of circumstances and with all kinds of goals achieve skills, knowledge, and opportunities through deliberate practice and sustained effort. Each day you have the opportunity to choose how you will invest your time. Here's to doing your best and being your best!

. . . .

Journaling Exercise: Compound Interest

Michael Simmons, Cofounder and CEO of Empact

One of the greatest forces in this world is compound interest. To leverage this force, we need the patience and focus to invest in every moment to be the best we can be for the long term. Although each individual investment may be invisible in the moment, its fruits are seen by all.

Investments in the invisible assets of character, knowledge, relationships, and reputation pay better interest rates than any bank that has ever existed.

Compound interest makes the seemingly impossible go to possible to probable to inevitable.

Looking at the average of other people and choosing one's destiny based on that average demonstrates a lack of understanding of this basic principle. Similarly, looking at your number one role model who has beat all the odds as an anomaly whose accomplishments cannot be copied demonstrates no knowledge of compound interest.

Look at anybody who has achieved greatness, and you'll surely find years and decades of investments that no one else saw.

I have faith in myself because I understand compound interest—I have for over a decade—and I continue to be willing to invest. I know that all of the big things in my life that I'm appreciative of stem from trying to be my best in all areas at all times.

Journaling Questions

- Have you been investing your time or having it spent for you? Why?

- What kind of returns would you like to see on your time investment?

- What is one action you can take today to start to be more conscious of how you're investing your time?

• •

Notes

1. I will make reference to some scenarios in my coaching clients' lives. Certain names have been changed or omitted to respect their privacy.

2. Lisa Johnson Mandell, "Your Job Can Kill You: Long Hours = Heart Attack." AOL, Inc. Available at: http://jobs.aol.com/articles/2011/05/17/your-job-can-kill-you-long-hours-heart-attack.

3. Heidi Grant Halvorson, *9 Things Successful People Do Differently*. Boston: Harvard Business Review Press, 2011.

CHAPTER 2

BREAK FREE

Overcoming Crippling Emotions

*People change what they do less because they are given
analysis that shifts their thinking than because they are
shown a truth that influences their feelings.*

—JOHN KOTTER AND DAN COHEN, *THE HEART OF CHANGE*

The Boston Marathon Limper

Again, again, and again, Jim had visualized one foot then the second cross-
ing the finish line of the Boston Marathon. He could imagine the whole
scene that would follow with vivid detail: his legs quivering from the
hard exertion of hours of running, his torso doubled over as he gasped
for breath in a violent effort to quench his body's thirst for oxygen, and
rivulets of sweat coursing down the contours of his face before dripping
off the jutting precipice of his chin.

Jim had memorized every positive affirmation known to distance
runners and rehearsed them with the faithfulness of the most ardent of
worshippers. He had eliminated all other distractions from his life so
that he could invest all his disposable time in training. He had researched
how long it takes for a runner at his fitness level to prepare for the Boston Marathon and had looked into other races where he could meet his
time qualification of three hours and 10 minutes. He had studied different routines and mapped out how the extra running and training could
fit into his schedule. He had even joined a running club and intentionally

connected with other motivated runners in his area. Oh yeah . . . he also had some running gear that made him look pretty awesome (at least in his extremely humble opinion of himself).

Jim was ready to win or at least finish. Right? Well, . . . almost. Except for the fact that every time he laced up his shoes and attempted to run, a sharp pain shot from his right knee up into his thigh, causing his leg to crumple like a soldier wounded by enemy fire. Instead of the exhilaration of completing a grueling long-distance run that perfectly corresponded with his meticulously planned training schedule, Jim resorted to the sheepish limp, hop, hop, limp, hop, hop of the injured runner in a matter of seconds.

Had he prepared for glory? Absolutely.

But could he achieve it? No—or at least not until he attended to the crippling pain in his knee that thwarted his glorious plans.

Why Emotions Matter (No Matter What You Think)

In the realm of time investment, our life is the marathon, and our emotions—such as overwhelm, guilt, or fear—are our crippling injuries. Left unaddressed, they can completely sabotage all other change efforts.

Depending on your personality type, the idea of attending to your emotions in the process of time investment change may seem marvelous or odious. If you tend toward experiencing the world through your feelings, giving yourself the freedom to express your emotions seems natural. (An exception to this rule happens when you experienced some sort of trauma or were brought up in an environment where the general culture or particular people discouraged or prohibited the expression of emotions. Even though, by nature, you experience your emotions quite easily, by nurture, you were taught to repress or suppress them.)

But if you tend toward the analytical, just-tell-me-the-facts sort of orientation toward the world, plunging into the ominous forest of feelings seems suspicious at best, terrifying at worst. "Why should I have to consider things such as feelings, which I don't even have?" you scoff. "I'm not a weakling influenced by such trivialities. Just tell me what to do, and I'll do it."

Oh really? Just tell you what to do, and you'll do it? If everything were really that simple, why are you reading this book? Why haven't you "just done" what needs to be done with your time management?

As John Kotter and Dan Cohen share in *The Heart of Change*,[1] a book based on over 200 interviews done by Deloitte Consulting, "Behavior change happens in highly successful situations mostly by speaking to people's feelings."

In *The Happiness Hypothesis*,[2] Jonathan Haidt describes the relationship between emotions and rational thought in this manner:

> *Our emotional side is an Elephant and our rational side is its Rider. Perched atop the Elephant, the Rider holds the reins and seems to be the leader. But the Rider's control is precarious because the Rider is so small relative to the Elephant. Anytime the six-ton Elephant and Rider disagree about which direction to go, the Rider is going to lose.*

This is why before we jump into time investment principles, we need to take some time to uncover and then address crippling emotions. To help you with identifying these potentially nebulous feelings, I've provided clues in the form of observable red flags that something may lurk under the surface. You may find that you recognize signs of one or two or all of these emotions! That's natural and normal. At different seasons in your life, you will experience various combinations of emotions, and these can even vary on an hour-by-hour basis.

In each section I also outline harmful thought patterns that can create the emotion and helpful thought patterns that can release you from it. If some of the "What's Happening?" or "Red Flags" sections sound strangely familiar, you may want to post the "Helpful Thought Patterns" in a place where you can see them on a frequent basis. You want to saturate your brain with a new way of thinking that will, in turn, create a new, better emotional response. (We'll also cover more techniques for changing your mental wiring in the section on affirmation in Chapter 3.)

Then you can try out the essential actions to break free from the control of these crippling emotions. If they help, fantastic. If not, try some

other combinations until you find the right cure. These exercises will empower you to consciously take back control of your time investment instead of being driven by subconscious compulsions.

When You Can't Keep Up: Overwhelm

What's Happening?

Overwhelm happens when you feel disproportionately matched to what is happening in your environment. Most often this occurs in two areas: speed and quantity. With *speed overwhelm*, it feels like the world is whizzing by you like a Corvette convertible breaking new speed records, whereas you can barely putt along at the minimum speed limit. This sort of overwhelm happens in environments where you must respond quickly to requests, such as when you work in a direct customer support area, or in a position where you have short deadlines, such as journalism. On a regular basis, you are asked to produce within a short interval of time, and you can't keep up with the pace. With *quantity overwhelm*, you still have the feeling of not having the capacity to keep up. But this sort of overwhelm tends to center around the quantity of deliverables required from you instead of just the speed at which you need to process them. For example, if you work as a professor, this could look like needing to write an extensive article for a research publication, review students' papers, sit on committees, and update the course material. You may have months to complete these projects, but the sheer volume of requests feels like more than you have to give.

> ▶ **RED FLAGS:** Responses to overwhelm generally fall within two categories: shutting down to the point where you do anything but something productive (i.e., instead of working on your paper, you watch television) or constantly pushing yourself in a desperate attempt to keep up despite the impossibility of the situation (i.e., repeatedly working long hours, staying up late trying to get things done, and rarely—if ever—taking a moment to sit still). In both cases, you feel out of control and incapable of ever keeping pace with the demands put on your time.

Breaking Free

TABLE 2.1 *Key Mental Shift: Overwhelm*

HARMFUL	HELPFUL
I must do whatever it takes to keep up with my environment.	I can choose to modify my environment and my response to my environment so that I feel comfortable with the pace and quantity of what is asked of me.
Not being able to keep up is my fault and means that there is something wrong with me.	I can improve my efficiency but ultimately need to accept and embrace what is reasonable for me to accomplish.

Essential Actions

- **Start with yourself.** Instead of trying to conform yourself to your outer world, work on adapting your environment to your inner world. This means asking yourself how much you can take on right now and then limiting your commitments accordingly. Pay close attention to the upcoming chapter on priorities, and consider cutting out all activities that don't align with your highest goals. Robert Epstein, a psychologist and self-help author, did a 3,000-person survey and discovered that planning was the best stress management technique. You can reduce stress by "fighting stress before it even starts, planning things rather than letting them happen," Epstein says. "That means planning your day, your year, and your life so that stress is minimized."[3]

- **Allocate time carefully.** In addition to determining what you will do, you also want to clarify for yourself how much time you will invest in each activity. If you know that you have five hours to complete three items, you should predetermine how much of that time you want to budget to each activity, whether they include household chores such as dusting, grocery shopping, and doing laundry, or work items such as answering e-mail, completing a proposal, and writing a recommendation. Then, as you begin each activity, think about how much time you have to complete it, and ask yourself, "Within this amount of time, how much can I reasonably accomplish?" The time block acts as a filter to help you set realistic expectations on the quantity

and quality of your work. For instance, if you only have 30 minutes to spend on your entire grocery shopping trip, you may only pick up staples such as milk, bread, and fruit and leave shopping for a fancy dinner party to another day.

- **Take a break.** Although it may seem counterintuitive to cease activity when you feel like you have far too much to do, rest gives you the perspective that allows you to determine priorities and set reasonable expectations. It also gives you the emotional capacity to move forward without burning out. Every day you should have at least a short break, whether it's listening to music in the car, reading before going to bed, or having a conversation with someone who makes you laugh. Choose something that you find refreshing, and give yourself permission to be fully present in that moment.

When You Feel Dull and Listless: Ambivalence

What's Happening?

When you experience ambivalence, you have simultaneous conflicting feelings toward a person or thing. This could mean a love-hate relationship with a major project that you know will do great things for your career, but you also know will require immense amounts of time and effort. It also could look like really wanting to step out and try activities such as learning to dance or practicing a new language but at the same time wondering if you will trip over yourself and end up looking foolish. Or you

▶ **RED FLAGS:** Ambivalence can surface in different forms. In one form, it creates a sort of overall malaise because the two strong opposing emotions have canceled each other out. You feel emotionally dull and potentially mentally fuzzy. You have trouble deciding how to focus and lack ambition to do much at all. You can't pinpoint anything in particular that's wrong, but you also don't feel particularly enthusiastic about anything. In a second form, you may on a conscious level have a very clear emotion in one direction, such as wanting to come home in time for family dinner. However, when you go to take the action, such as leaving work earlier, something holds you back or creates what psychologists would call *approach-avoidance*. The same thing can happen with such areas as being on time. If you consistently say that you feel horrible that you always arrive late, yet you can't bring yourself to make the changes to arrive at the designated hour, you may be experiencing ambivalence.

could desire to spend less time working but worry that having free time in the evenings will leave you lonely and painfully aware of your lack of meaningful relationships.

> Another related topic that you may want to explore if this sounds like you is *cognitive dissonance*, which goes beyond competing emotions to include simultaneously holding conflicting ideas, beliefs, values, or emotional reactions.

Breaking Free

TABLE 2.2 *Key Mental Shift: Ambivalence*

HARMFUL	HELPFUL
There is nothing really wrong, so I just need to push myself to do what needs to be done.	If I'm experiencing doubt, hesitation, mental debates, or other signs of internal dissonance, I have some conflicting thoughts or feelings.
Stopping to consider anything unrelated to directly taking action is a waste of time.	It's essential to address the internal conflict before moving forward.

Essential Actions

- **Identify the sides.** Your first goal in this kind of situation is to raise both sides to your conscious mind. You can do this in a number of ways, such as the next time you feel internal conflict, stopping and asking yourself, "What exactly is causing me to hesitate?" At first, you may not have words to describe what is happening, but you may notice a physical sensation, such as a tightening in your throat or a knot in your stomach. Focus on that sensation for a bit, and see if you can identify any emotions or whether any thoughts come to mind. To garner further clues, carefully observe your actions to see what you avoid or move toward. Also, if you feel comfortable, you may want to ask for an outside opinion on what others observe about your actions and about what they think may be at the root of your ambivalence.
- **Address issues.** Once you've identified the opposing forces, you need to listen to each side and determine what, if anything, you can do to

address the concerns. In some cases, you may have the opportunity to quiet the opposition. In others, you will need to proceed with the two still not having come to a peaceful truce. (*Warning:* At this point, you may feel worse than you did before because you no longer have repressed strong emotions. This discomfort is actually a good sign that you're breaking up emotional scar tissue and putting yourself in a place where you can operate in a healthy, congruent manner.)

• **Go with your gut.** When you can't rationally eliminate your internal emotional conflict, you can activate your gut instinct to help you to decide how to move forward. Frenk van Harreveld, a social psychologist at the University of Amsterdam who studies how people deal with ambivalence, shared in a *Wall Street Journal* article entitled, "Why So Many People Can't Make Decisions,"[4] that if he can't decide on a conscious level, "he flips a coin, and if his immediate reaction when the coin lands on heads is negative, then he knows what he should do."

When You Are Constantly on Edge: Fear

What's Happening?

A real or perceived threat to someone or something important to you creates a sense of fear. This anxiety can come from dangers to tangible items such as your job, your marriage, or your house or intangible items such as respect, status, security, love, self-worth, and comfort. Either way, you feel that the world is not safe and that you may suffer a loss or get hurt at any moment. Ironically, this emotion not only surfaces in situations we would typically classify as negative but also occurs in seemingly

> ▶ **RED FLAGS:** To an outside observer, the symptoms of overwhelm and fear may appear very similar. Someone attacked by fear typically will shut down and avoid menacing situations or throw himself or herself into such situations in a frantic and frenzied manner. But to the person experiencing the emotion, fear creates a different internal state. When you find yourself in a place of fear, you literally feel trapped and on edge. You will tend to be jumpy and overreact to any question or request either by retreating like a scolded puppy or lashing out in defensiveness. You also may notice these physical signs: constriction in your throat, queasiness in your stomach, difficulty sleeping, increased muscle tension, eye twitches, appetite changes, and racing thoughts.

positive situations that still threaten us in some way. A promotion, a new relationship, an overseas vacation, or a stretch project can endanger our confidence and sense of security. This is why it's just as plausible to have the fear of success as the fear of failure.

Breaking Free

TABLE 2.3 *Key Mental Shift: Fear*

HARMFUL	HELPFUL
The world is a dangerous, unstable place, and I am alone and vulnerable.	I cannot prevent all change and insulating myself from new inputs limits my opportunities.
I must preserve the status quo because any change signals a personal attack against me and what I hold dear.	I can take the appropriate actions to prepare for the future and then trust that in the moment I can respond appropriately to whatever happens.

Essential Actions

- **Verbalize the fear.** By simply stating out loud exactly what you fear, you can start to decrease its power. Much like the monster under the bed that as a four-year-old you absolutely *knew* would eat your toes disappeared as soon as a flashlight shone on it, externalizing what you fear often scares it away or at least makes it look much less intimidating. I recommend talking through fears with a trusted adviser or at least writing them down and then saying them out loud.

- **Harness the motivation.** Sometimes clarifying your fears helps you to define where you need to make a plan and follow it. For example, you may have a fear that you will not meet your sales quota for the month. Instead of letting that fear taunt you, you can turn the negative emotion into positive action that will lead to you making your numbers. This could look like deciding to contact 10 new prospective clients a day and following up with all your existing contacts this week. If fear starts to creep up once you make the plan and are taking the appropriate action, you can silence the fear by saying to yourself, "I have a plan, and I'm following it. I can focus on doing what is within my control, and I don't need to be afraid of the results." As a quote

attributed to Mark Twain goes, "Courage is not an absence of fear. It is acting in spite of it."

- **Find unconditional love.** In many business and academic environments, your psyche is inundated with these sorts of messages:
  - You must achieve and produce to have value.
  - If you stop pushing, you risk others surpassing you.
  - You are what you do.
  - If you perform at a lower level, you are less of a person.

  Given these messages, it's only natural that you would feel fear of not measuring up or becoming obsolete. To help grow your sense of intrinsic self-worth, spend time with groups of people, such as your family or faith community, where you ideally experience unconditional love and acceptance and receive these sorts of messages:
  - You are of value simply because you exist.
  - No one can take your unique and special place in the world.
  - You are important regardless of what you do, earn, accomplish, or own.
  - Your intrinsic worth is not correlated with variable outside circumstances.

When You Blame Others: Frustration

What's Happening?

When you believe that the power to improve your situation or how you feel lies within others' control, you end up bitter, resentful, and downright frustrated with those around you. You believe that they should take the blame and take the action to fix whatever displeases you. Also, some part of you glories in the fact that your verbal grenades cause them to experi-

> ► **RED FLAGS:** It seems like the whole world has conspired against your happiness. Every driver pulls in front of you. Every telephone operator puts you on hold. Every service person is incompetent. You feel like no one understands you and no one cares for you. If you yell at someone, you don't apologize because they deserved it. You swear often. You don't forget . . . or forgive. You tend to leave small tips because the wait staff could have done better. You feel jealous of others' success and feel infuriated when you don't get what you believe you are entitled to receive.

ence some of the pain that torments you. Below this prickly surface, however, lies a deep, chronic sense of insecurity. You have unresolved issues or unfulfilled needs. And since you feel powerless to address them yourself, you try to control or coerce others into taking care of them for you.

Breaking Free

TABLE 2.4 *Key Mental Shift: Frustration*

HARMFUL	HELPFUL
Other people control my experience of life.	I can decide how much of an influence others have on my life and on my mental and emotional state.
I am powerless to directly improve my situation, so I must attempt to meet my needs indirectly through coercing and controlling others.	If I am dissatisfied with my current status, I can take action to improve my situation and my response to it.

Essential Actions

- **Claim your power.** The first step to breaking free of frustration involves releasing yourself from victim status. If the idea that you have any sort of control seems incomprehensible to you, I want you to try this exercise for a day: Every time anything happens and your eyes narrow and your mind flits to who you can blame, I want you to ask yourself, "What can I do about this situation?" Then answer the question in a way that puts you in control of the next step independent of what anyone else chooses to do or not do.
- **Meet your need.** If a fellow commuter cuts you off on the way to work, you can choose to slow down to increase your sense of security. If a coworker sends you an e-mail that makes you angry, you can ask him or her to clarify so that you can better understand the message and then go for a run to blow off steam. If a housemate eats everything in the refrigerator, you can go out for dinner. Whatever happens, you want to practice responding in a way that satisfies your needs instead of waiting for others to take care of them for you.
- **Assume good intent.** Most people don't purposely take actions to annoy you unless they truly have an insidious bent. More often than

not, they simply didn't think about how what they did or said would affect you, or they had thought about it and had come to the wrong conclusion. Instead of assuming bad motives, start by assuming good intent by saying phrases to yourself such as, "They probably didn't think about . . . " or "I know they didn't mean to hurt me . . . " or "From their perspective, I can see why they. . . ." Giving others the benefit of the doubt is not invalidating your experience of the situation or excusing their behavior. But it is decreasing your negative emotional response, empowering you to take action, and putting you in a better place to dialogue effectively if you do need to talk through an offence.

When You Must Meet a Standard: Guilt

What's Happening?

When the instruction manual for your life consists of a long list of dos and don'ts, and you have a huge sense of responsibility to fulfill your proper role in the world or else, you have a scenario that will lead to guilt. This emotion arises when your actions do not perfectly match up with your standards. This incongruence then brings fear that you have done something wrong and will experience some sort of penalty or be proven personally inadequate. Guilt can arise both from not doing enough to "earn your keep," "prove yourself," or "make the grade" and from not doing enough to make someone else happy if you have assumed the rescuer role in the life of someone with a victim mentality.

> ▶ RED FLAGS: Hiding information, lying about situations, coming up with excuses, avoiding eye contact, not responding to messages, and inflicting self-deprivation as a form of penitence all signal guilt related to not meeting certain standards for yourself. Allowing people to violate your boundaries, never saying, "No," always putting other individuals' needs above your own, denying yourself basic self-care such as sleep, and overextending yourself financially in order to make others happy are signs that you suffer from guilt owing to a sense of over-responsibility for others.

Breaking Free

TABLE 2.5 *Key Mental Shift: Guilt*

HARMFUL	HELPFUL
If I don't meet my standards or others' expectations of me, I'm a failure and absolutely worthless.	I have nothing to prove.
There is no excuse for not performing to the proper level or for disappointing others.	I can do my best to meet certain standards. But if I do not meet them, it does not mean that I am a failure; it just means that I did not get certain results from my actions.
I cannot rest until I've done everything, and I can never forgive myself for mistakes.	If I do feel that I've made a mistake, I can learn from the situation and ask for and accept forgiveness from myself and others.

Essential Actions

- **Identify the standard.** Clarify for yourself exactly what standard, either explicit or implicit, you feel you must achieve: Is this a company policy? A moral code? A family tradition? Once you've clarified what type of standard you use to measure yourself, question it. Think very hard about whether you agree with this rule and whether you feel that you should evaluate yourself against it or not.
- **Clarify your responsibility.** Take time to identify which parts of a circumstance were in your control and which parts fell outside your control. With those outside your control, such as the weather, unexpected emergencies, or other people's emotional responses, practice releasing responsibility by imagining a sort of invisible shield between the circumstance and your conscience. The magic words to deflect the arrows of guilt are, "_____ was *not* my fault. I did what I could to plan and to accommodate other people's needs. But I'm not to blame for factors outside my control that meant everything didn't turn out perfectly and everyone wasn't completely happy."
- **Accept forgiveness.** If you truly have done something that violated a personal standard and caused harm to others, apologize to them, do your best to make the situation right, ask for forgiveness, and if

they give it to you, accept it. Also, regardless of whether they extend forgiveness to you, you can choose to forgive yourself by admitting that you regret what you have done and releasing yourself from the bondage of self-condemnation and self-loathing.

When You Fear Being Known: Shame

What's Happening?
Unhealthy shame results when you feel that you do not meet cultural or social standards and have put yourself in an irreversible condition of dishonor or disgrace. Many times this emotion goes beyond feeling that you have done something wrong to feeling that you *are* something wrong. In this state, you believe that you are so deeply flawed that you must do everything possible to hide your true self from the world. You believe that if people knew who you really were, they would turn away in horror and could not possibly have any empathy or compassion for you. Therefore, you must hide, pretend, and avoid situations where people could get close enough to you that they would really know who you are. *The Psychology of Shame: Theory and Treatment of Shame-Based Syndromes*[5] explains shame in this manner:

> *Because shame is central to conscience, indignity, identity, and disturbances in self-functioning, this affect is the source of low self-esteem, poor self-concept or body image, self-doubt and insecurity, and diminished self-confidence. Shame is the affect that is the source of feelings of inferiority. The inner experience of shame is like a sickness within the self, a sickness of the soul.*

▶ RED FLAGS: If you feel a need to cover up your true self, to pretend, to avoid close relationships, to run from yourself, to repeatedly move, or to have no cracks in the surface of a perfect exterior, you may suffer from shame. Other micro-level signs of this emotion include blushing, looking down, staying silent, and assuming a bent-over posture meant to make you look smaller.

Breaking Free

TABLE 2.6 *Key Mental Shift: Shame*

HARMFUL	HELPFUL
I am fatally flawed.	I am accepted, loved, and wanted right now—just as I am.
If others knew who I really was, they would reject me.	Others can know and love me.
I must wear a mask, project an image, pretend, and always be in control.	I can be my true self and reveal who I am, especially to those closest to me.

Essential Actions

- **Accept yourself.** Before you can move forward, you need to choose to accept yourself right now, just as you are. This means facing what you most fear people will find out and saying or writing out something to the effect of, "Even though I _____, I completely accept myself." This allows you to look the part of you that you most fear in the eye and give him or her a huge embrace of unconditional love and acceptance. Through this act, you create a more coherent, unified self.

- **Change groups.** If you feel a strong sense of shame for who you are based on the people with whom you spend time on a regular basis, you may need to evaluate what's really happening: Are people actually judging you? Or do you simply believe that they are criticizing you? If you are experiencing true judgment that you feel is inappropriate and is causing you to be ashamed in an unhealthy manner, you may want to consider changing the people with whom you associate on a regular basis.

- **Open up.** Work on developing relationships with a few people whom you can trust. Then take the risk of gradually sharing more and more of your true self with them. One of the best ways to heal from shame and to defeat the lies that torment you is to have tangible examples of the opposite being true. When people love, accept, and respect you even after knowing the "true you," your shame can gradually disappear, and you can experience inner wholeness.

I hope that as you progressed through this chapter you gained insight into some of the emotions that may have stood in the way of you making the most effective time investment choices. Going through these action steps will feel uncomfortable—and potentially even frightening. But you can choose to be different, to show yourself compassion, and to create a different future for yourself.

However, if as you progressed through this chapter you started to feel more uncertain instead of more free, you may want to check out books such as *Feeling Good: The New Mood Therapy*[6] or *Ten Days to Self-Esteem*,[7] by David D. Burns, M.D., that take a much more thorough look at overcoming depression, anxiety, and perfectionism. You also may want to consider seeing a counselor, therapist, psychologist, or psychiatrist if you believe that your condition has a physiological component or if you would like to further explore the potential root causes behind these emotions.

· ·

Journaling Exercise:
Ten Tools I Learned for Feeling Good
Michaela, a time coaching client who learned how
to balance a full-time job and going to school
without feeling constantly overwhelmed

I really like that the university forces me to grow. And this semester, even with lingering self-doubt, hurt, and fears, I have seen improvements I never thought I could make. I don't want to stop taking classes next year because there are still issues I want to resolve, and this hard, stressful situation is somehow accelerating the growth in this area. I want to do a lot more stuff in my life, and it will not get easier, so I want to gain the skills to deal with it.

The university is not the problem at all (as you probably know); it is the way I treat myself and how I deal with it. It would be easy to quit, get back in my comfort zone, and think that things will vanish. But I know they will reappear as soon as I take on the next challenge. So why not deal with it now?

I want to find a toolbox to deal with these stressful situations. So far I have learned through coaching with you (in no particular order):

1. Feeling and validating the emotions that are coming, meaning taking them seriously, and then choosing what I want to do. When I feel deprived, alone, and exhausted, I probably *am*, and it is not a dumb feeling that does not know how much there is still to do. The best way to deal with it is not rationalizing and fighting it. It is doing something for me that I think I am missing, like taking a nap, relaxing a few hours, meeting friends, or doing something sporty. I always thought I was too tired and exhausted for these activities. But now I realize that these things are giving me energy and not taking it from me.

2. Doing something for my body is extremely important for my energy, for my mood, for my health, and for my feelings. I cannot postpone it. This also helps me get things done in a better way instead of preventing me from doing the things I "have" to do.

3. It is okay to feel anxious, to not want to feel like a beginner, to be afraid of failure, and to be afraid of rejection. It is okay to feel these things and still choose to do the thing I fear nonetheless. It is also okay to allow myself to stop if I want to.

4. It is not about the end result. It is about the process. My focus is much better put on enjoying and improving the process and not focusing on the result. The result will come if I do the process. A happy life is not a life with a lot of results but with a lot of happiness in the process. Learning, for example, can be fun.

5. It is not helpful to think about all the things that there are to do or how little time is left. These thoughts are not giving me motivation, happiness, determination, or energy. They are just putting me in a depressing mood where I don't want to do anything. I am capable of doing a little step right now, if I choose to do so. However, it is totally my choice. And little steps amount to even the biggest accomplishments. I cannot change the past, and in this moment, I cannot change the future. I just can do something right here, right now.

6. It is enough being me. I don't have to be fast or especially smart or funny or self-confident. I can make progress just as I am.

7. I can love myself regardless of what is happening in my life.

8. I can be relaxed and calm at any time. If I focus on being relaxed, no to-do list, no failure, and no deadline can change that peace. My emotional state is determined by where my attention goes.

9. I don't have to judge success based on results. I can evaluate success as doing what I planned and committed to do. The results are just a by-product that happens or doesn't happen depending on lots of factors. I can move forward step by step and cheer myself along.

10. If I don't achieve certain results, I will be 100 percent on my side. I will comfort myself. I will not beat myself up. I will remember that I did what I could do without killing myself, and I will think of a way to move forward. My safety comes from knowing that there will not be a terrible, terrible thing that happens if my results don't measure up and I seem to have failed. I will go on unharmed. I will not judge myself by the results. I will evaluate whether I keep doing something. That is all I can do, move forward, and I am allowed to feel successful each day by appreciating just that.

Journaling Questions

- Did any of these tools resonate with you?

- If so, which ones and why?

- How could you start applying these 10 tools or some of the essential actions to overcome the crippling emotions in your life?

. . . .

Notes

1. John P. Kotter and Dan S. Cohen, *The Heart of Change: Real-Life Stories of How People Change Their Organizations*. Boston: Harvard Business School Press, 2002.

2. Jonathan Haidt, *The Happiness Hypothesis*. New York: Basic Books, 2006.

3. Marina Watson Pelaez, "Plan Your Way to Less Stress, More Happiness," *Time*. Available at: http://healthland.time.com/2011/05/31/study-25-of-happiness-depends-on-stress-management.

4. Shirley S. Wang, "Why So Many People Can't Make Decisions," *Wall Street Journal*. Available at: http://online.wsj.com/article/SB10001424052748703694204575518200704692936.html.

5. Gershen Kaufman, *The Psychology of Shame: Theory and Treatment of Shame-Based Syndromes*, 2nd ed. New York: Springer, 1996.

6. David D. Burns, *Feeling Good: The New Mood Therapy*. New York: Avon Books, 1999.

7. David D. Burns, *Ten Days to Self-Esteem*. New York: HarperCollins, 1999.

CHAPTER 3

STAY STRONG

Empowering Mental Exercises

*Now if you are going to win any battle you have to do one thing.
You have to make the mind run the body. Never let the body
tell the mind what to do. The body will always give up.
It is always tired in the morning, noon, and night.
But the body is never tired if the mind is not tired.*

—GEORGE S. PATTON, 1912 OLYMPIAN, U.S. ARMY GENERAL

The Road to Arua

Disturbances. That was the term used by the bus driver to explain why a quick stop at a gas station had turned into a 30-minute break and then a three-hour stay complete with chickens (both on and off the bus), longhorn cattle (only off the bus), and a thunderstorm.

I took the unexpected delay fairly calmly at first. I had flown in late the night before to Uganda from the United States via Istanbul. For much of the day, though, I still had the shiny new glow of the wonderful first stage of culture shock, where everything seems absolutely marvelous. I was chipper and peaceful as I closely followed along behind my traveling companion on the multiple forms of intracity public transportation that we took prior to getting to the intercity bus. I kept my chin up and gaze confident when people yelled at me, "Mzungu! Mzungu!" (something that local men, women, and children tend to shout at foreigners at any time). I took it in stride when the bus stood still at various towns, and villagers held

up food to the windows, more or less a rural African equivalent of drive-through fare. Some of the offerings looked welcoming—such as cold bottles of soda pop—others looked a bit less appetizing to my Western eyes, such as fish still wearing their original skin and kept lukewarm by the day's sun.

Even when we initially hit the disturbance, I remained unperturbed. I had brought a book, and given that in my "normal" life I rarely have the chance to indulge in hours of reading, I took advantage of the opportunity. (It's the time coach in me! I couldn't just sit and stare into the distance like many of my fellow travelers clustered in groups outside the bus, keeping a watchful eye on their children or slowly chewing their snacks from the gas station convenience store.)

After a delay of over three hours—one hour due to the driver deciding that the bus was in fact having a real disturbance versus a minor hiccup and two and a half due to the time it took for another bus to drive from the capital city of Kampala to where we had gotten stuck—we were back on the road to Arua. Because the bus company owners had incurred extra expense in sending a vehicle to rescue us, they made up the cost by doing what the locals call *overloading*. This meant that the capacity of the bus no longer matched the number of seats but instead became how many men, women, children, and chickens could squeeze in without preventing the door from shutting. Our stops became more frequent as we took on more and more passengers until the center aisle contained a stream of people—standing, sitting, or squatting in an attempt to get comfortable. It was also necessary for the bus to drive at a slower rate given that no street lamps illuminated the road after nightfall, and people or animals could pass over at any moment.

Our travel to Arua in the northwestern part of the country stretched out from an anticipated 6 hours to an actual 10 hours given the change of circumstances. Fortunately, though, owing to mobile phones, we could keep in touch with our hosts. They were there to greet us when we forced ourselves and our bags over, around, and through the mass of people and popped out of the bus like salmon escaping from a dam.

By the time we arrived at our resting spot for the next few nights, the jet lag and the wear of the day's journey had risen to my consciousness. I went from merely feeling exhausted to feeling downright sorry for myself when I got the explanation about how to check for cockroaches before

using the toilet at our lodging. The gas station where we sat for most of the afternoon had not had an actual toilet, so I knew I should be grateful. But being a spoiled American, it was hard. I wasn't used to the masses of people. I wasn't used to the reactive approach to bus repair. I wasn't used to the sounds, smells, and bugs. I had trouble sleeping that evening because every noise made me wonder if I was safe and if some mighty mosquito had penetrated the netting shielding my bed from malaria attacks.

The next day I had the opportunity to explore the compound run by ORA Uganda to serve what it calls "vulnerable children." On the facility grounds, the staff members of the nonprofit take care of orphans and children with illnesses such as HIV/AIDS when their families cannot tend to them properly. The compound contains community training facilities, an office building, sleeping quarters, a playground, a plant nursery weeded by a wandering goat, cooking facilities, and supply huts.

I walked over to the swarm of children around the swing set and said hello to one of the little boys who spoke a bit of English (the children learn English in school but primarily speak their local tongue). I asked about what he was learning in his classes. He told me that he had been learning about organs and named a few, such as his heart, his brain, and his stomach. I told him that he had a very good brain to remember all those things. In response to the compliment, his mouth stretched into a tooth-baring grin, and his eyes lit up and expanded with a surge of pride.

Given that I seemed to have treated their comrade well, other children began to come up to me, asking me questions, showing me how they could do little acrobatic feats, and dangling from the trees overhead. We sang songs together, complete with arm motions, and the children showed off their strength by moving a sack of rice so big that it took four of them to get it to flop end over end.

But most of all, they *radiated* joy.

They were away from their families. They had potentially life-threatening diseases. Their clothes were dirty and worn from their boisterous outdoor play. They most likely had no money to their names. They definitely didn't have mobile phones or computers. But, in my opinion, they were the ones to be admired, not pitied. They truly had it all in that they obviously delighted in their lives, delighted in their friends, and delighted in all the good that they did have instead of dwelling on what was not.

One of the biggest lessons I took away from my visit to Uganda was the gift of gratitude. It's not having more or being more that makes you happy—but *fully enjoying the present*. From that trip, I vowed to even more actively strengthen my positive mental muscles. If those children can live lives abounding with joy, I can too.

Play-Doh and Bouncy Balls

In Chapter 2, we talked about how to let go of negative emotions that try to hold you down and pull you back from effective time investment. In this chapter, we move on to how to take a proactive approach to increasing positive emotions in your life, such as joy, hope, confidence, and peace.

These techniques make you less vulnerable to pain caused by negative forces—no matter what your circumstances—and give you a greater ability to push them out if they do intrude. Here's why:

- When practiced regularly, these mental exercises take you from a place of your emotional state having the consistency of Play-Doh, which is extremely impressionable and splats on the floor when dropped, to one of a bouncy ball, which very rarely dents and springs up immediately after a fall.
- When used as a strategy to counteract crippling emotions, these tactics push out the negative by filling your mind with so much positive that there's no room for anything else.

For best results in improving the effectiveness of your time investment, I recommend that you make these exercises part of your daily routine. At minimum, you should keep them on hand to help you out when you find yourself struggling to get motivated and move forward. I love this truth, shared from one of the pull-off pages of a day-by-day calendar: "Quieting down is a mind-set, not a set of circumstances. There are plenty of people with relatively few actual emergencies to deal with, who are freaked out and stressed almost all of the time. There are others who deal with extraordinarily stressful things, but who are able to take most of it in stride." I believe that one of the best ways to become part of the latter group is through practicing the following techniques.

Increase Your Joy: Gratitude

What It Is

At the core, gratitude is about appreciating what you have, who you are, and where you are—right here, right now. Instead of taking things for granted, comparing yourself to others, or looking at the perceived lack, gratitude involves noticing and being thankful for the present.

Why It Matters

Having a bigger house, receiving a promotion, being in a relationship, making more money, losing weight, or achieving any other aspirations will not in and of themselves make you feel happy. Being able to enjoy, appreciate, and be content in your circumstances brings the positive emotional state.

TABLE 3.1 *Key Mental Shift: Gratitude*

HARMFUL	HELPFUL
When I _____, then I will be happy.	I am grateful for what I have and where I am now.
I deserve what I have, and I'm entitled to things being how I want them.	I am very thankful and feel fortunate for everything that I have in my life.

Gratitude Strengthening Exercises

- **Appreciate small things.** As my story about my trip to Arua revealed, many of us take for granted luxuries that we see as absolute necessities: running water, electricity, and indoor plumbing, among other things. When I returned to the United States and went to the grocery store, it literally felt like some sort of nirvana given the variety of food, the lack of mud, and the absence of flies hovering overhead. When you start getting really upset about life, make a list of everything that you enjoy—walking, talking, laughing, watching a TV show, and so on—and start each line with the phrase, "I am thankful for. . . ." As Michaela so wisely stated at the end of Chapter 2: "A happy life is not a life with a lot of results, but with a lot of happiness in the process."

- **Find the good.** Even the most difficult of circumstances have some good in them or some good that can come from them. For instance, if you find your work stressful, you can be thankful that you have a job and that you are learning perseverance. If your children drain your energy, you can be grateful that you had the ability to have kids and appreciate that they live in your home. As the late entrepreneur and motivational speaker Jim Rohn said, "Success is not so much what we have as it is what we are." Often the most difficult of situations develop our character to the greatest degree.

- **Go serve someone.** When you live in a "bubble" of people who look like you, do what you do, and have as much or more than you have, your perspective of what's normal can get dramatically skewed, especially if they have a high level of affluence. To regain a balanced perspective, sign up to give meals to the homeless, volunteer at a nursing home, or travel to a developing country. Your appreciation for all you have will increase in light of this broadened worldview.

A Story of Rediscovering Gratitude from Teri,
a Time Coaching Client

Since September, when I took a three-week vacation—something I never even dreamed of doing—a lot of things have happened. I took a step back after the three months of time management you lead me through, and. . . . Oh my! Where do I begin?

Vacation was fantastic! I did a lot of nothing, so it seems, but I did do plenty. I met new people. I took my first real yoga class— amazing! I took Spanish lessons, read, rested, walked nearly every day for more than two miles, got a massage weekly, and more.

When I got home, reality hit, and I didn't adjust well to the woes of my "job" life. I cried the first couple of days when customers on the phone were unhappy, and I couldn't help them directly. My mom said it was hormonal. I didn't think so.

I went to my chiropractor, and he said something profound to me: "There are people who would love to have the job you have. I

don't always want to do what I do every day, but I thank God for
every patient that comes in my door. I am grateful for the blessings
that come in every day. You should be too." So I changed my attitude
in short order, and by Thursday of the first week, one day after my
appointment, I had the best day of the week. The following week
was better, and every day since has been better. I am happy for every
moment I am working here. I pray to have a smile on my face with
each caller and person who enters my lobby.

Increase Your Hope: Optimism

What It Is

Optimism or, as some people like to call it, *positivity* has a number of
appropriately rosy definitions. The Mayo Clinic[1] defines it as "the belief
that good things will happen to you and that negative events are tem-
porary setbacks to be overcome." And Merriam-Webster puts it this
way: "an inclination to put the most favorable construction upon actions
and events or to anticipate the best possible outcome." Basically, in this
state, you believe that life is good, and even if it's not—it will get better
very soon.

Why It Matters

Some people (usually pessimists) look down on people who are optimists.
They believe that this cheery outlook has no correlation with the hard
truths of life and is simply a form of denial and an avoidance of engaging
in the proper mountain of worry. The habit of always assuming the worst-
case scenario tends to come more naturally to some personality types. It
also seems to have woven itself into the DNA of some groups of people
who have generations of experience with extremely trying circumstances.
However, realistic optimism, as described in the following excerpt from
9 Things Successful People Do Differently,[2] leads to many tangible benefits,
including better health, increased productivity, and even a longer life span.
In one study referenced in a *New York Times* article entitled, "A Richer
Life by Seeing the Glass Half Full,"[3] "Adults shown to be pessimists based
on psychological tests had higher death rates over a 30-year period than

those who were shown [to be] optimistic." Those who choose to think positively not only have a better life experience, but they also literally have more life to experience.

TABLE 3.2 *Key Mental Shift: Optimism*

HARMFUL	HELPFUL
The future is grim, and I will always be disappointed.	Good things await me, and I'm so excited for the future.
If I meet a challenge I cannot overcome on the first try, it's all over. I'm doomed.	If I hit a roadblock or have a setback, I can try again with a new strategy or more effort. If I keep at it, I can succeed.

Optimism Strengthening Exercises

- **Dream in color.** Dare to let yourself think about the best-case scenario and to imagine yourself living it out. Instead of hedging your bets, saying you don't really want things, settling for what's practical, and being modest, risk sounding ridiculous in your aspirations. Allow yourself to get excited about all the possibilities in the future. By believing that you can achieve great things, not only do you increase your chance of doing so, but you also get to enjoy the pleasurable dopamine rush regardless of what happens in the end. Dopamine, a hormone that gives you a sense of euphoria, is highest in anticipation of a reward, not in the actual achievement of it.[4]
- **Control the controllable.** Indulging in the right kind of optimism gives you the ability to hope that all your hard work will pay off in the end. This sense that what you do has a purpose and will bring a reward dramatically increases your ability to face challenges with gusto and seek out opportunities to succeed. When you look on the bright side, you can also dare to cheer yourself on at each small step, knowing that it brings you closer to your final victory.
- **Be tenacious.** In *Breaking Murphy's Law: How Optimists Get What They Want Out of Life—And Pessimists Can Too*, the author shares that she and other researchers have found that optimists are motivated and positive and attack problems directly instead of giving up in the

face of difficulty. They focus on finding solutions, not bemoaning challenges.[5] Practice reframing every challenge as a chance to grow, and surround yourself with people who believe in you and your dreams so that you can keep at it.

Explanation of Realistic Optimism from 9 Things
Successful People Do Differently[6]

> *Realistic optimists believe they will succeed, but also believe they have to make success happen—through things like effort, careful planning, persistence, and choosing the right strategies. . . .*
>
> *Unrealistic optimists, on the other hand, believe that success* will *happen to them—that the universe will reward them for all their positive thinking, or that somehow they will be transformed overnight into the kind of person for whom obstacles cease to exist.*

A study on weight loss, referenced in the same section on "realistic optimism" as the preceding excerpt, revealed the expected truth that women who believed that they could lose weight were more likely to do so. But the study also provided a surprisingly strong case for realistic optimism: Women who thought that they could succeed without great effort lost 24 pounds less than those who believed that the process would be difficult. Having confidence in their abilities *and* acknowledging the challenges ahead brought the greatest success.

Increase Your Confidence: Affirmation

What It Is
Whereas gratitude allows you to enjoy the reality around you and optimism gives you hope for good things to come, affirmation gives you confidence in yourself. Affirmation involves two parts: The first step is consciously letting go of ways of thinking that make you believe that you are incapable of changing and doing what you were meant to do in your life. The second step is replacing those limiting thought patterns with empowering ones.

Why It Matters

As the article, "6 Clues to Character,"[7] from *Psychology Today* explains, "Cognitive behavioral therapy is founded on the fact that we consistently engage in automatic patterns of thinking about experience, of which we are generally unaware, that pitch us into positive or negative mood states." This means that a propensity toward depression doesn't just relate to whether or not you encounter difficult situations—everyone faces adversity. Instead, depression results from distorted interpretations of the experience based on assumptions about it and beliefs about yourself.

For example, someone in need of practicing more affirmations to increase her self-confidence might interpret not receiving a response to an e-mail she sent regarding a job opportunity in this way: "How could I have possibly thought that I had any hope of getting that job? Obviously, the hiring manager just hates me and thinks I'm annoying and doesn't want to respond to my e-mail." Someone with a more confident, positive sense of self more likely would mentally interpret the same scenario in a very different way, such as: "I haven't received a reply to my e-mail, which must mean the hiring manager is very busy. I think I could be a great fit for the job, so I'll follow up again in a few days via e-mail. Then, if I don't hear back, I'll find a phone number and make a call. I really want to make sure to have a personal connection with this hiring manager and to demonstrate how I really want this position and am willing to work hard to get it."

For those who need affirmation the most, I know that this concept can seem the least reasonable. How can you say nice things about yourself, which at this point you don't believe are true? And how can just repeating positive affirmations make any difference in your life? To address the first question, you can act in a certain way, and the repetition of certain actions will gradually transform you into the kind of person you desire to become. For example, you can practice the drums every day and become a drummer, or you can practice patience every day and become a patient person. In the same way, repeatedly thinking about yourself in a certain way, such as, "I'm a confident person" or "I'm able to respond calmly under stress," gradually transforms you into the type of person who embodies those qualities. Just as the negative "mental videotapes" have caused you to act in a certain way in the past, positive programming is an essential part

of doing what you want to do differently in the future. Affirmations in a sense "free" the elephant we talked about in the last chapter to do what the rider tells it to do.

This sort of mental conditioning has quantifiable benefits not only in terms of putting you into a positive emotional state but also in terms of improving behavioral performance. At the 2011 annual meeting of the Society of Personality and Social Psychology,[8] researchers from many universities, including Carnegie Mellon and Stanford, shared views on the powerful impact of self-affirmation on key behaviors, including handling stress, losing weight, performing academically, and recovering following a health trauma such as breast cancer. Self-affirmation was shown to reduce stress response, increase self-control, and decrease defensiveness, all incredibly powerful tools in the process of lasting behavioral change, including effective time investment.

TABLE 3.3 *Key Mental Shift: Affirmation*

HARMFUL	HELPFUL
I am a loser and a failure.	I am successful and a winner.
I am not _____ enough or I'm too _____, so I'm incapable of success and unworthy of good things.	I am enough, and I'm capable of doing well and worthy of receiving good.

Affirmation Strengthening Exercises

- **Notice your thoughts.** In the blink of an eye and often completely subconsciously, we react to circumstances with thoughts that reflect our beliefs and our interpretations of the meanings of events. As the preceding example shows with the e-mail that didn't receive a reply, it's not the situation that dictates our emotions and our corresponding next actions, but our thoughts about the situation. The next time you notice yourself doing something you don't want to do (such as randomly surfing the web when you should focus on a big project) or when you experience a crippling emotion, such as fear or guilt, work backward to identify the initial trigger event and then the corresponding thoughts. By replacing your mental response to key triggers, you can dramatically reduce unproductive emotions and actions.

- **Depersonalize the attack.** One of the most difficult parts of strengthening your affirmation mental muscle is that the lies can seem . . . so true. To help you start the process of change and open yourself up to believing something different about who you are, it helps to change the negative reproaches to "You" statements instead of "I" statements. For instance, when you hear the statement, "I always procrastinate," you can rephrase it as, "You always procrastinate." This properly classifies it as an outside attack that you can question and then replace with the truth. If you would like to take a more in-depth look at this "voice-fighting" technique, I recommend that you read *The Worry-Free Life: Take Control of Your Thought Life by Weeding Out the Bad and Nurturing the Good!*[9] or check out my blog post, "Shut Up and Cast Out the Voice of Overwhelm," which provides a brief synopsis of this strategy (www.reallifee.com/voice-of-overwhelm).

- **Dwell on good.** As much as possible, you want to saturate your mind and your environment with positive messages about who you are and what you can do. This could mean writing affirmations that are meaningful to you and then reading them every day, posting them around your living or work area, making a recording of yourself or someone you love saying these affirmations and then listening to them regularly (some people even listen to recordings while they sleep), choosing positive songs that encourage you to fill your day, reading inspirational material, and spending time with people who build you up. Basically, you want to reprogram your mind so that instead of repeating critical thoughts over and over and over again, it can't help but say good things about you. This is the equivalent of getting a good song stuck in your head that affirms who you are and encourages you in what you're doing.

Affirmations in Action in a Mom of Three's Life

When I first began working with a single mom who had gone back to school to finish her bachelor's degree, she found almost everything about her schedule a struggle from morning until night. Getting up to help her oldest son make the bus on time seemed almost impossible, focusing in the morning so that she could go to an aerobics class before heading to her college campus rarely happened, and in the evenings, she and her children

ended up cramming to finish school work, leaving them all exhausted the following day.

Everything in life just felt so . . . hard—kind of like trying to wade through chin-high water instead of skipping along the shore.

As our time together progressed, we discovered that she had a great deal of trouble feeling good about her abilities because she had a number of critical voices ringing in her head. These came from having grown up in a family that cared about her and wanted to help but rarely respected her opinion on how she wanted to be assisted. The aftermath of a nasty divorce and an ex-husband who filled her with fear almost every time they interacted also had left a serious gap in her confidence. The messages that she had received most of her life and that played over and over again in her head were: "You're not capable. You are dependent. You don't have a right to your opinion. You aren't good at making decisions. You are a follower, not a leader. Your opinion is not important. You need to do as you are told and stay silent."

During our time together, my client was able to start to question these negative thoughts and to replace them with positive affirmations about herself and her abilities. I distinctly remember one session where she told me that she just kept repeating to herself, "I'm confident and capable. I'm confident and capable."

It may seem like a small change, but simply repeating the truth about who she was and what she could do freed my client to take the actions that would allow her to become the kind of woman she wanted to be. In class, she began taking more of a leadership role on group projects, with her ex-husband she spoke up more and set better boundaries, with her parents she explained her preferences instead of being convinced otherwise, and she took control of her time so that she not only could finish her degree but also could excel in her school work.

Affirmations changed her mind and her life, and they can do the same for you.

Increase Your Peace: Mind Time

What It Is

I was going to call this section "Meditation," but I felt like that unnecessarily limited the scope, so I came up with the term *mind time*. What do I

mean by this term? Any sort of activity where you set aside time to get lost in your thoughts. That could mean more traditional forms of meditation, where you clear your mind of ideas or perhaps focus on a particular mantra. That could mean prayer, where you communicate with a higher power. That could mean what I call *mental processing*, where you think through all that just happened, how you felt about it, and whether you need to do anything with it going forward. Or that could look like dreaming, where you project out to the future. Whatever it looks like, it's giving yourself time to think, either in a completely focused manner or by layering it onto some other activity, such as walking or driving on a deserted stretch of highway.

Why It Matters

Everything we covered in Chapter 2 on emotions and this chapter on mental exercises hinges on whether you actually give yourself time to think about your current thoughts, your emotions, what you would like to change, and what actions you will take. If you need more incentive, keep this in mind: Meditation reduces stress, increases focus, and actually can change your brain quantifiably. According to a research study done by scientists at Massachusetts General Hospital, an eight-week mindfulness meditation program lead to an increase in gray-matter density in the part of the brain responsible for learning and memory and a decrease in the area responsible for anxiety and stress responses.[10]

All sorts of "mind time" exercises, including prayer and processing, give you the ability to gain perspective and to choose your response to what happens to you instead of succumbing to an automatic stress response. In a *Newsweek* article entitled, "Tired of Feeling Bad?"[11] Richard J. Davidson and Sharon Begley share how their research has shown that emotional resilience depends a great deal on the general activity in the prefrontal cortex and the number of neural connections between the prefrontal cortex, responsible for the highest of higher-order cognitive activity, and the amygdala, involved in negative emotions and distress when we feel threatened. And the great news is that owing to the brain's ability to change its structure and function, known as *neuroplasticity*, by investing time in the right kinds of mental exercises, you can change your automatic response to stressful situations.

TABLE 3.4 *Key Mental Shift: Mind Time*

HARMFUL	HELPFUL
Focusing on my thoughts instead of my actions is a waste of time.	My thoughts play a critical role in my ability to perform the right actions.
It's impossible to slow down my mind or focus.	It may not come easily or naturally to me, but I can choose to spend a small amount of time each day on mind time.

Mind Time Strengthening Exercises

- **Make it ritual.** Mind time will never seem urgent unless you've gone far too long without it. At the point where you feel like you need to completely rebuild your brain—like a fried computer hard drive— you've waited too long. It's much better to do this sort of mental reset on a daily basis. To help this occur naturally, pick a regular trigger event, such as getting up in the morning, going to bed at night, or commuting to work, when you take time to think, to pray, to meditate, or to do whatever other mental exercises calm you down and give you a sense of perspective. Check out this article on my blog for some additional tips on how to make this happen: www.reallifee.com/ time-for-prayer-meditation.
- **Do what works.** I think people too often get hung up on the fact that they need to do prayer, mediation, or any other mental exercises in a certain way. Do what works for you, and worry less about the means and more about the ends. This might mean that your best thinking happens while you are running or driving or dusting or as you lie in bed in the morning after hitting "Snooze." Or you may need to have a much more structured environment where you attend a group yoga class or a faith group. If you're lost and need more direction, look up a book, take a class, or ask an expert. However, if your current mindfulness exercises work well for you, simply keep at them.
- **Start small.** If you really struggle with focus for even a short amount of time, begin with a minute or two of mind time, and then gradually increase the length or frequency. I have one time coaching client who put an app on his phone that chimes every hour and reminds him to

check with himself whether or not he is doing something important. You can do something similar to remind yourself to take a moment to breathe or to think something positive or simply to step back and ask yourself, "Why am I doing what I'm doing?"

An Excerpt from "The Joy of Quiet" by Pico Iyer[12]

The only way to do justice to our onscreen lives is by summoning exactly the emotional and moral clarity that can't be found on any screen. Maybe that's why more and more people I know . . . seem to be turning to yoga, or meditation, or tai chi; these aren't New Age fads so much as ways to connect with what could be called the wisdom of old age.

. . . .

Journaling Exercise: Taking Back Control as an Entrepreneur

Joanna Lindenbaum, Founder of
Soulful Coaching for Busy Women

I really wanted to share Joanna's story because I find that so many people who previously had a healthy mind-set about work tend to make a turn for the worse when they become entrepreneurs. All of a sudden, we go from recognizing that work has boundaries and that we need to invest in other parts of our lives to allowing our business to consume every waking hour. I personally needed to overcome this problem when I started my first business in 2005 without any sort of coherent schedule. (Go to www.reallifee.com/meet-elizabeth for the full story.) I mastered my time investment habits, which led to a better life and a better business, and so did Joanna. I want you to take our stories as examples that remind you that owning a business doesn't have to mean killing yourself to succeed. Here's Joanna's story of taking back control of her time and her life:

My whole life I had been an "over-responsibility person," meaning that no matter what, I was going to do whatever it took to make sure everyone around me was happy, satisfied, and

okay. This intense need of mine to be responsible for everyone and everything stemmed from growing up with a perpetually ill mother who depended on me and needed for me to be the adult in the family. Making sure that everyone else was happy was a major piece of my identity and how I perceived my value in the world.

When I opened the doors to my business in 2007, my over-accommodating self was in full swing. I had no concept of boundaries *at all.* I worked eighty-plus-hour work weeks; scheduled sessions with clients whenever they wanted one (including 6 a.m. and 11 p.m.); traveled all over Manhattan, Brooklyn, and Queens to have those sessions (instead of deciding that clients must travel to me); spent hours daily on client follow-up via e-mail; and charged as low as $15 per session (and my travel time—I'm not kidding!).

You know what the result was? I was thoroughly exhausted, sick much of the time, isolated from friends and family . . . and pretty much broke! I took poor care of myself and allowed others to dictate practically everything I did. I felt depressed, worn out, and unhealthy.

Finally, one day I realized that there was no way to go but out and that I must learn how to stand up for myself. From that moment on, I began to show up for my life as my own advocate and stopped allowing everyone else's needs to come first. I started working on my boundaries and systems, and now I'm proud to share that

- I work no more than 25 hours most weeks.

- I continuously raise my rates and charge what I'm worth.

- My yearly earnings are in the multiple six figures.

- My clients receive *more* value than ever before.

- I have time and energy left over for myself, my family, and my life.

- I have a team that supports me in every aspect of my business.

- I take self-care 100 percent seriously and receive regular massages, acupuncture, etc.

Today I am successful in my career, feel soul-satisfied, and am surrounded by loving family and friends.

Journaling Questions

- Did you notice the power of affirmation in Joanna's transformation?

- What areas of your life seem to constantly challenge you, and what mental exercise might offer the correct antidote?

- How will you make one or more of the mental exercises in this chapter a regular part of your routine so that you experience more joy, hope, confidence, and peace?

. . . .

Notes

1. Jane E. Brody, "A Richer Life by Seeing the Glass Half Full," *New York Times*. Available at: http://well.blogs.nytimes.com/2012/05/21/a-richer-life-by-seeing-the-glass-half-full.

2. Heidi Grant Halvorson, *9 Things Successful People Do Differently*. Boston: Harvard Business Review Press, 2011.

3. Jane E. Brody, "A Richer Life by Seeing the Glass Half Full," *New York Times*. Available at: http://well.blogs.nytimes.com/2012/05/21/a-richer-life-by-seeing-the-glass-half-full.

4. Matthias Rascher, "Dopamine Jackpot! Robert Sapolsky on the Science of Pleasure." *Open Culture*. Available at: www.openculture.com/2011/03/science_of_pleasure.html.

5. Jane E. Brody, "A Richer Life by Seeing the Glass Half Full," *New York Times*. Available at: http://well.blogs.nytimes.com/2012/05/21/a-richer-life-by-seeing-the-glass-half-full.

6. Heidi Grant Halvorson, *9 Things Successful People Do Differently*. Boston: Harvard Business Review Press, 2011.

7. Harra Estroff Marano, "6 Clues to Character," *Psychology Today*. Available at: www.psychologytoday.com/articles/201104/6-clues-character.

8. spspmeeting.org/archive/SPSP2011_Program.pdf.

9. Terence J. Sandbek and Patrick W. Philbrick, *The Worry-Free Life: Take Control of Your Thought Life by Weeding Out the Bad and Nurturing the Good!* Sacramento, CA: Green Valley Publishing, 2008.

10. Christie Nicholson, "Meditation Correlated with Structural Changes in the Brain," *Scientific American*. Available at: www.scientificamerican.com/podcast/episode.cfm?id=mediation-correlated-with-structura-11-01-22.

11. Richard J. Davidson and Sharon Begley, "Tired of Feeling Bad? The New Science of Feelings Can Help," *Newsweek*. Available at: http://www.thedailybeast.com/newsweek/2012/02/19/tired-of-feeling-bad-the-new-science-of-feelings-can-help.html.

12. Pico Iyer, "The Joy of Quiet." *New York Times*. Available at: www.nytimes.com/2012/01/01/opinion/sunday/the-joy-of-quiet.html?pagewanted=all.

THE 3 TIME
INVESTMENT SECRETS

CHAPTER 4

SECRET #1

Clarify Action-Based Priorities

*Most people struggle with life balance because they haven't
paid the price to decide what is really important to them. . . .
The key is not to prioritize what's on your schedule,
but to schedule your priorities.*

—STEPHEN R. COVEY, AUTHOR OF
THE 7 HABITS OF HIGHLY EFFECTIVE PEOPLE

Please Rob Me

"Hey Rob, I forgot my lunch, so I'm just going to take $10 out of your wallet to go grab a sandwich," commented Mike, an outgoing coworker, as he grabbed the cash and ran.

"Hmmm," Rob thought, "I guess I won't have enough money for lunch today because the deli only takes cash. But at least Mike told me this time. That's really nice of him. The last time he took lunch money, I didn't make the discovery until I sheepishly stood in front of the register with my ham and cheese sub with no onions and extra pickles swaddled in white paper sitting between me and the scowling cashier. That was sooooo embarrassing."

Rob turned back around to his computer and started typing furiously. He had learned that if he got into some sort of flow state, he didn't notice his stomach growling on the frequent occasions when others had taken his cash.

Just as he began to get immersed deeply into the preparation of a document for the next day, the phone rang. "Rob, here," he answered.

"Hi Rob, it's Alicia," said a high-pitched voice on the other end of the line.

"Oh, well hello Alicia," Rob replied in his typical congenial manner. "How are you?"

"Well, not so good," Alicia sighed. "Do you know those outlet malls near my house? The ones with the *amazing* designer deals?"

"Why, yes," Rob answered. (He didn't shop much, but he had remembered seeing a billboard advertising the stores.)

"Well . . . , they were just having these incredible end-of-season deals on Prada shoes and Gucci sunglasses and Hermès purses, and I just couldn't contain my enthusiasm," Alicia explained. "I had maxed out my credit card on my last trip to Vegas, so I just used one you had given me a while back. I knew you wouldn't mind. I just wanted to call and say thank you for always being so generous. Okay, bye."

After Alicia hung up, the drone of the dial tone buzzed in Rob's ear for a few moments as he processed what he had just heard. His sister, the fashionista, had just purchased a new wardrobe on his credit card. "Well, I'll have to make sure that I check the balance before Saturday," Rob thought. "I want to be sure there's enough left for me to take my wife out to dinner and maybe get her some flowers. I sure do appreciate her."

Ever the diligent worker, Rob shifted his focus back to the task at hand and tried to put any worry about Alicia from his mind. "She's had a tough week with getting a bad haircut and all, and I know how important proper layering is to her."

Just then an e-mail notification popped up from his boss. The subject line read, "Year-End Bonus." "Exciting!" Rob thought. "I was thinking I would use my bonus to put a little more money in the kids' college fund and maybe even to have a real family vacation. It's been a few years since we all could get away and just enjoy one another."

The e-mail read:

Hi Rob,

Hope you're doing swell. I just wanted to let you know once again how much I appreciate your great work. You've really gone the extra mile to stay late and work extra to get things together for our

year-end reports. Also, you did a really stellar job on covering for me during the two weeks I was in Hawaii.

I really appreciate how you're just such a team player and so eager to do what it takes to make everyone happy.

So . . . you know that photo of the boat that I showed you—the 30-foot yacht? Well, I thought it would be just perfect to take with me on my trip to Greece in a few months, and they were running this special deal where if you buy before the end of the year, you get a significant discount.

And since you're such a nice guy, I didn't think you would mind if I just didn't give you a bonus this year and instead put it toward the boat.

I knew you would understand, and I'll be sure to send you a signed postcard (or at least bring an unsigned one back to the office).

Sincerely,

Rich

Crestfallen, Rob turned back to his computer with a little less gusto than before. The hunger had turned from a gnawing feeling to more of a light-headedness, and a little part of him felt disappointed about having his hopes dashed once more. "I guess I won't be able to do something nice for my family after all," Rob sighed. "Definitely no chance to get that new mountain bike I admired last week at the store. I wonder if it's still possible to get a new bike chain for a '92 model?"

In an effort to revive himself so that he could make it to the end of the day, Rob shuffled over to the water fountain. When he bowed his head down to take a drink, he put out his hand to brace himself against the wall because he felt a bit faint from low blood sugar.

"Rob!"

Startled, Rob righted himself and quickly swiped his hand across his face to brush away the water droplets that had splattered across his nose.

"Rob!"

Looking around, Rob saw Sherry and Joe approaching him with their usual strident confidence. It looked like the dynamic duo had a plan, and he was part of it—like it or not.

"So Rob," Sherry began, with a glance up at her companion in persuasion, "Joe and I were just brainstorming how we could be sure to have all the sponsored tables at our hospital gala sold within the next few days."

"And Rob," Joe interjected with a side smile at Sherry, "We remembered how you had children that had been born at the hospital and that you had purchased a ticket to the gala last year. So we naturally assumed that you would be delighted to sponsor a table to make sure that we look really good when we go to our committee meeting on Friday."

"Since you came to the event last year," Sherry continued. "We already had your debit card information, and we just took the liberty of taking the $1,500 from your account. We'll be sure to send you a receipt for the portion that is tax deductible."

"Thanks for being such a great supporter of our community," Joe said with a slap on Rob's back.

"We just could not do this without you," Sherry concluded with a grin.

Then they strode off down the hall, leaving Rob dumbfounded. "$1,500?!" Rob exclaimed internally, "That's a mortgage payment. How will I explain this to my wife?"

Do you feel infuriated at how people treated Rob? I did just writing the piece. How could people treat him that way? Why didn't he stand up for himself? But here's the point: If you're not effectively investing your time in your top priorities, you may be getting "Robbed" every day. Do you:

- Allow coworkers to schedule unnecessary meetings on your shared calendars?
- Give extended family members permission to ask you to do anything at any time?
- Say "Yes" to every request from your boss, even if it costs you evenings and weekends?
- Never turn down requests from volunteer organizations or other committees?

If so, you're allowing other people to spend your time for you instead of investing it for yourself. This is actually *worse* than allowing other people to spend your money for you because your time is quite literally your life. The only way that you can take back control is to really clarify your action-based priorities and to relentlessly focus on them.

Secret #1: Clarify Action-Based Priorities

Here's the truth: Time is limited. Because it's a finite resource, the only way to achieve more success with less stress is to invest it in what really matters most to you, that is, your priorities. This is why Secret #1 is *clarify action-based priorities*. Let's break down the three parts:

Clarify: *To free from confusion and make understandable.* Just as Rob allowed the people around him to spend his money instead of having decided on his priorities and put in the appropriate boundaries, the same thing can happen to you with your time. Also, many things also are specifically designed to steal your time. Facebook, Twitter, blogs, e-mail, apps, TV shows, and a plethora of other technologies compete for your attention. Unless you make specific choices to limit their pull, you'll succumb to their tantalizing promises of distraction, fun, and mental stimulation for more than the proper time allocation. But when you plan and when you make intentional decisions about what you will or will not do, you have the opportunity to clarify and reclarify your priorities.

Action-based: *Supported by something you do.* This portion of secret #1 allows you to go from clarifying what's important to you to defining exactly how you will invest your time in alignment with your priority. For example, let's say that you decide that family is a priority. You could make that priority action-based by coming up with these supporting to-do items:

- Be home for family dinner four nights per week.
- Attend children's sporting events on the weekends.
- Spend one night a week enjoying quality time with my spouse.

By making your priorities action-based, you gain these benefits:

- You can know whether or not your time investment reflects your priorities.
- You can have a framework for making decisions.
- You can do other things without guilt, such as working late one night a week or going out for drinks with friends.
- You can avoid tension between you and your other family members as to which actions constitute making family a priority.

To help you see this concept in action, here are a few more topical examples:

- **Exercise:** Go to the gym three times per week, park in the far parking lot, do 10 push-ups a day.
- **Management:** Have monthly one-on-one meetings with direct reports, provide feedback quarterly, answer boss's and direct-reports' e-mails within 48 hours.
- **Rest:** Turn off the phone after 10 p.m., in bed by 11 p.m., no work on Sunday.

Priorities: *Something given or meriting attention before competing alternatives.* Priorities come as a natural result of the truth I mentioned before: Time is a finite resource, and the only way to achieve more success with less stress is to invest it in what really matters most to you.

No matter how efficient you become, you will never have the capability to do everything. By living a life in synch with your priorities, however, you can feel good about what you do and don't do and how much time you allocate to each activity. This is a huge part of overcoming many of the crippling emotions we covered in Chapter 2.

I can't overemphasize the importance of ensuring that you honestly define and "own" your true priorities. If you live your life according to someone else's definition of success, you will feel absolutely miserable, no matter how much you seem to achieve. Also, in owning your priorities, make sure that you make room for other people, such as your significant other, children, coworkers, employees, and friends, to own theirs. Just because you only need six hours of sleep doesn't mean that someone else is wrong or lazy for wanting eight. Just because you would rather go surfing on a Saturday morning instead of working on a special work project doesn't mean that someone else isn't happily living in line with his or her priorities by logging into work on the weekends.

Own your priorities, but don't judge others.

Your Personal Definition of Success

We are the most satisfied and fulfilled and able to unleash our greatest potential when we are aligned with not only what we want to do but also

TABLE 4.1 *Key Mental Shift: Action-Based Priorities*

HARMFUL	HELPFUL
If I'm just more efficient, I can do everything right now.	I have a limited capacity, so I need to make choices about what's most important and let go of the rest.
If this is important to someone else, it should be important to me.	I can choose to invest my time in what I genuinely find meaningful and satisfying.

who we want to be. Right now, I want you to open yourself up to the process of discovering your *personal definition of success*. This is not about what your boss wants, how "society" defines success, what your friends desire to do, or imitating anyone else (even me!). To help with this process of self-discovery, I have a series of questions for you to answer below. Pick a time and space where you'll be free to let your thoughts wander, and indulge in some *mind time*. If you enjoy journaling, write out your answers. If you prefer to think while exercising, take these to the gym. Or if you need to "talk out" your ideas, make this part of a discussion with someone you can trust to support you, and be open to your dreams—no matter how "impossible."

A Few Notes Before You Begin

- If you don't get through all these questions, it's okay (just pick your favorites!). The important thing is that you set aside time to focus on what you would like to have happen so that you can clarify action-based priorities.
- If you're confused as to why I mention the feelings involved when you do certain activities, here's a bit of explanation:
  - First off, we usually don't want to achieve or have something; we want the feeling that comes from achieving or having something. Some common examples: a promotion (feelings of importance, respect, authority, and job security) or a relationship (feelings of love, being valued, safety, and trust).
  - Second, to discover your personal definition of success, you need to honestly evaluate what emotions certain things create in you.

Pay attention to the reality of what makes you feel happy versus what you think should make you happy, and you'll be much better off. So often we feel dissatisfied in life because we ignore alternative opportunities that could bring us to our desired feeling, or we accomplish something and realize that it didn't create the internal state that we hoped to achieve. For example, maybe in your situation, a promotion makes you feel stressed, trapped, and resentful because you can no longer do the creative work you love.

- If you think you must settle, I encourage you to consider this wisdom from Gretchen Rubin, author of *The Happiness Project* and *Happier at Home*, who wrote about this topic in a blog post called, "Do You Fall into This Happiness Trap? The False Choice."[1] In this article, Gretchen notes how we can often trick ourselves into thinking that we only have two specific choices. She then goes on to explain that we're tempted to superficially limit our options to avoid feeling overwhelmed by too many possibilities and to make it easier to categorize one alternative as high-minded and reasonable and the other as not. But here are her words of warning: "Although false choices can be comforting, they can leave you feeling trapped, and they can blind you."

Move into these exercises from a place of possibilities, not limitations. You might be able to have much more of what you truly want with much less sacrifice than you might think if you take the time to clarify and go after your personal definition of success. For a downloadable .pdf of these questions, go to www.reallifee.com/tib.

Start Pondering

- Describe a time when you felt really successful.
- What activities or situations fill you with energy?
- What motivates you?
- What causes you stress?
- Are there any traditional measures of success (e.g., many direct reports, large salary, lots of travel) that don't fit with your personal definition of success? If so, what are they, and have you been feeling badly for not achieving them?

- What makes you afraid either about maintaining the status quo or about changing something?
- Who do you consider a professional role model, and why?
- Who do you look up to as a personal role model, and why?
- When do you feel most at ease and natural both personally and professionally?

Write Priorities

- List and rank the different aspects of your life in order of importance.
- Write out the specific actions you would like to see happen in relation to those priorities. For example, if friends are a priority, a related action could be one get-together with friends per week.
- Describe the benefits you hope to achieve from making your priorities a priority. In other words, what will success with effective time investment look and feel like? For example, when I wrap up work on Friday afternoon knowing that everything else can wait until Monday, I will feel peaceful and happy.
- What are you willing (or not willing) to sacrifice?
- How fast do you feel you need to achieve your goals?

If these questions stumped you, try out the following exercises to get inside your subconscious mind and help you to discover what you truly want:

- Imagine that you're an old man or woman sitting on a porch reminiscing about your life over the last 70 years. Describe what has made you proud, sad, disappointed, or elated about what you did (or did not do) and who you are and were.
- Pretend that a reporter is interviewing you 5 or 10 years from now. She asks you these sorts of questions about the past few years: What have you learned? What's happened? What would you change?
- Picture a fairy godmother, a genie, or whatever other magical being you prefer, waving a wand and creating your dream lifestyle. What would happen? What would stay the same? What would change?

What would other people say? What would it look like, taste like, and smell like?

I encourage you to record your thoughts on at least a few of these questions in a place that you can refer back to on a regular basis. As you build your routines and assess your progress, you'll always want to check back to make sure that you stay true to your personal definition of success. You want to captain your ship, making course adjustments as the wind changes but ultimately ending up at the destination you chose in advance.

Priority-Based Decision Making

Clarifying action-based priorities gives you the ability to use them as a decision-making filter for your life. I thought Eric Farkas did a brilliant job of describing how this process works in his post, "How to Do a Startup on the Side and Not Lose Your Family,"[2] so I've included an excerpt here:

> *I've learned to go about making priorities by thinking about my life in this following manner:*
>
> *inner life → relationships → provision → employment → obligations → startup → enjoyment*
>
> *. . . I have my priorities, listed in my order of importance. Realizing that they are all related, I nevertheless run every opportunity through the priority framework, and ask the questions: Where does it fit? Given what's been going on in my life in the last couple of days/weeks/months, can I pursue this opportunity without harming something higher up the priority chain?*
>
> *For example, I enjoy playing soccer. My brother and his buddies regularly play on Saturday mornings at a high school not far from my house. Most weeks, given how busy things normally are, I would not be able to justify spending a Saturday morning away from my*

kids doing something like that. It doesn't contribute to anything above "enjoyment" in the priority chain, and whatever small "inner life" benefit I'd get by playing soccer would be negated by the harm it'd do to my relationship with my wife and children, knowing that dad had a free Saturday morning but spent it kicking a ball around instead of taking us out to breakfast.

There are times, however, when for some reason I've been able to spend a good amount of time with my kids during the week and taking a few hours to play soccer on a Saturday isn't a big deal. It's a play-it-by-ear situation. But most of the time, if I have free time, I try and spend it with my family instead of for myself.

I also have to turn down some legitimate provision opportunities as well because of the harm they'd do to my relationships. A full-time job and part-time startup take up a lot of energy, and adding something like a short-term consulting project to the mix, even though it may pay well, is something I can't do. In the last year, I've turned down three such opportunities.

Likewise, there are some jobs I wouldn't take because of the impact it'd have on my family life. Things like consistently long hours (in a day job) are a deal breaker for me. That might disqualify me for a job at many web startups, and that's okay with me.

Do you see how Eric has really clear priorities and owns them in his time investment decisions? Really beautiful. You can check out the entire post here: www.ericfarkas.com/posts/how-to-do-a-startup-on-the-side-and-not-lose-your-family.

I also hope that you see from this example that effective time investment doesn't have to look the same every day and that work-life brilliance doesn't only fall within the realm of a nine-to-five job with a half-hour lunch break.

One of my friends who is a brilliant entrepreneur, Zach Ferres, asked for my opinion on a super popular article in *Inc.* magazine entitled, "Why Working More Than 40 Hours a Week is Useless."[3] This article stated that research shows that consistently working more than 40 hours a week is simply unproductive. Here was my e-mail response to Zach's question:

In terms of the number of hours worked, I don't think that there's a magic number that works for everyone. In my experience as a time coach, I see that some people can work more than 40 hours and be just fine, and others need to work less than 40 hours.

Here are the key success indicators that I bring people toward that have less to do with quantity of hours worked and more to do with their quality of work and life:

- *I feel consistently energized and focused and engaged in whatever I am doing in the moment.*
- *My time investment is aligned with my priorities, so there is no feeling of guilt, overwhelm, or resentment.*
- *I have the proper time allocation within my work hours in terms of the type of work I am doing.*
- *I have the proper time allocation outside my work hours that includes physical/mental/emotional/spiritual health.*
- *My time investment is purposeful and proactive.*
- *I feel peaceful, in control, confident, and accomplished.*

My goal is that my time coaching clients can say, "Yes!" to all of these statements and be aligned with their ideal schedule, not to have everyone work a 40-hour workweek. I've found that people who consistently work (or claim to work) 55 or more hours a week are typically either procrastinating, not setting realistic expectations for themselves and others, not focusing on what's most important, and/or have poor boundaries and are allowing other people to spend their time for them. But not everyone needs to—or depending on their profession, can—work a standard 40-hour workweek.

Dynamic Priorities Model

Part of what sets apart my time investment secrets from more traditional time management philosophies is the recognition of these time truths:

- Priorities should be action-based.
- Overall time capacity is static.
- Life is dynamic.

This is why when you do daily and weekly planning in the time investment model, you not only come up with to-do items, but you also overlay them on your schedule so that you can have a clear idea of whether they fit within your 24 hours in a day and seven days in a week. We'll cover accepting your capacity more thoroughly in Secret #2: Set Realistic Expectations. For now, though, I want to share with you a model for understanding the interrelated nature of your priorities. I call it the *dynamic priorities model*. You can use this model to get perspective on both your overall life priorities and your priorities in a specific area, such as how you invest your work hours (see Figures 4.1 to 4.3).

Here's how it works: The very outer edges of the circles represent your time capacity. This is static. No one can have more than 24 hours in a day or seven days in a week. The rings represent your various priorities.

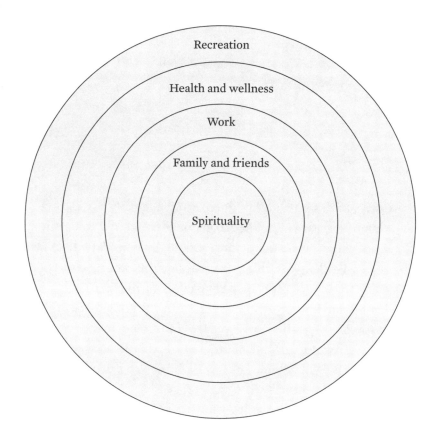

FIGURE 4.1 *Dynamic priorities model: Normal state.*

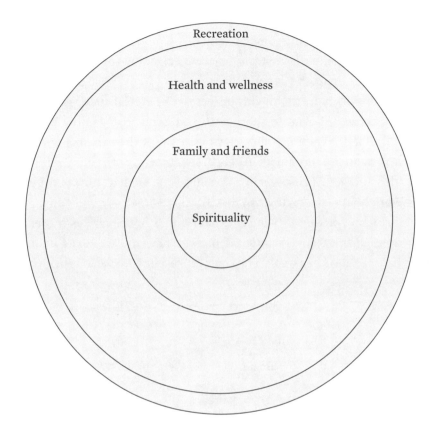

FIGURE 4.2 *Dynamic priorities model: Major illness.*

These always have some level of fluctuation on a daily basis. At certain times, though, specific rings will expand or contract in a more dramatic fashion (new child = wider family ring; serious illness – wider health ring; major project = wider work ring). As we accept this natural ebb and flow, we can come to terms with realistic expectations for what can fit in our lives right now and how investing more time in one priority means having less to give to another priority. If you apply this model on a micro level, let's say just in relation to your hours at work, this could look like more time preparing for a conference means less time to work on such "rings" as internal communications and e-mail processing.

Problems can arise in aligning your time investment with your personal definition of success when one or both of these situations occur:

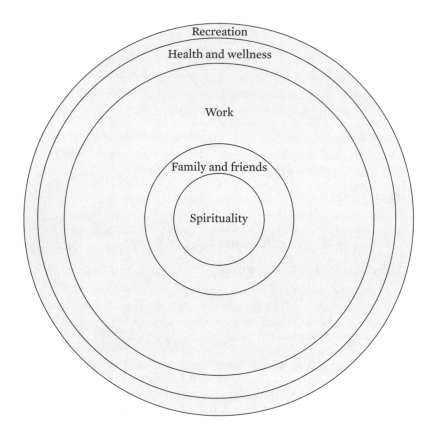

FIGURE 4.3 *Dynamic priorities model: Big work project.*

- Something that should sit in one of your top-priority center rings has popped outside the overall circle. For instance, maybe you never get enough sleep or you rarely communicate with your family.
- A ring hasn't fallen outside your overall circle, but it has gotten too thin, so your time doesn't have the proper allocation. Much like a river flooding its banks, a misallocation of time resources can lead to chaos.

To remedy the first difficulty, start placing the actions that make your top priorities your top priorities back into your schedule. This will cause lower-priority items to either drop off your schedule or constrict in width. To remedy the second difficulty, start to set up stricter boundaries, such as when you will or will not work, so that one part of your life doesn't consume an incorrect proportion of your time.

Balancing and Rebalancing

A key point to remember is that the act of balancing and rebalancing is a process and a journey, a privilege and a challenge. You can't flip a switch and know that you and your routines will run like clockwork indefinitely. Instead, you need to decide what "ideal" looks like for you and then start to develop the simple routines that reinforce your action-based priorities and realistic expectations. If you do this, you should find that you *consistently* invest in your priorities even if you can't *constantly* have life just as you would prefer.

TRUE IN TIME, TRUE IN FOOD

I love how Bethenny Frankel, TV personality, creator of Skinnygirl cocktails, and author of *Naturally Thin* and *The Skinnygirl Dish*, applies these same truths about choices and correct allocations to a healthy perspective toward eating in *A Place of Yes*[4]: "Don't deprive yourself . . . but don't overindulge, either. Understand that nothing in small portions is fattening, so you can have more of a good investment choice or less of a bad one. From now on, through the rest of your life, you will be faced with choices. Make the right ones for you."

When your life starts to feel out of control, it's important to know which of these types of challenges you're facing: a major systemic decision, a situational strategy change, or a tough phase or season. Then, like a tightrope walker tilting her pole, you can make the proper adjustments to get back in balance. The type of challenge you face will determine your next action steps:

A **major systemic decision.** When certain elements of your life make it impossible to live out your personal definition of success, you need to make a major systemic decision. In order to invest your time most effectively, be open to:

- **Changing jobs**—Leaving an environment that requires more hours than you want to work, that causes major stress, and/or that has too long a commute.

- **Switching businesses**—Moving away from something that requires more energy, more travel, and/or more extreme hours than you desire to give, such as working incredibly early or very late.

- **Letting go of certain customers**—Setting new expectations with clients or focusing on your best clients and allowing the time-sucking and stress-producing ones to fall away.

- **Cutting out particular commitments**—Reducing your number of activities or level of investment in them, for instance, stepping down from committees, attending fewer meetings, or changing your type of involvement (such as being a member of an organization instead of an officer).

- **Modifying goals or expectations**—Everything from deciding not to train for a marathon to keeping a less orderly home to choosing to take longer to finish your MBA. I'm not suggesting letting go of things that are really important to you but rather deciding when some less important items can slide so that you can stay in balance.

- **Monitoring your financial choices**—Purchase a smaller home, dwell in an area with a lower cost of living, sell a car, or pay down debt so that you have more choices in how much you work, how much you must make, and whether or not you can hire people to help.

Some of these decisions may take a great deal of time to think through and implement. (I'm not encouraging you to quit your job or shut down your business tomorrow!) But it is important that you're aware of and honest about certain areas of your life that keep you from consistently living out your personal definition of success. You should start looking for opportunities to modify your current situation or get into a new one so that you're not constantly fighting the system.

A situational strategy change. Sometimes you just need a change in strategy to regain balance in your life. It's not that you're doing an unsustainable number of activities or doing the wrong things. It's just that you need to practice more effective time investment strategies such as:

- **Setting or resetting your hours**—If you've started to work way too many hours or have swung the other way and barely do anything, it's time to step back and start over. Decide how much time you can realistically put into your work (or school or homemaking) right now and when you want to put in this time. Then, when you reach that day and time, start working and stop when you hit your end time. You want to develop the habit of starting and stopping productive tasks on schedule. (In Chapter 7, I go into more detail on exactly how to create these routines, and in Chapter 8, you can find out how to get accountability in place to encourage these habits.)
- **Consistent processing and planning**—Once you've gotten back on track with setting hours, it's time to get organized. This includes finding a system that you can consistently implement for handling the influx of information coming your way and sorting through what's most important and when it needs to get done. (See Chapters 6 and 7 for more specifics on daily and weekly processing and planning.)
- **Set or reset expectations**—Start to teach your clients and colleagues how much time you need to reasonably carry out their requests. Train them on how often and quickly you will respond to e-mail or other communications. If someone constantly interrupts you, start to set boundaries on when he can come to you and how you would like him to communicate with you. (See Chapter 5 for instructions on setting expectations.)
- **Make everything action-based**—If you feel unclear about what you need to do to invest more time in your top priorities, define some key actions that would ensure that you do more of what's most important and less of what's not. Then monitor those key actions on a consistent basis, ideally both daily and weekly.

A tough phase or season. Sometimes life is just a bit crazy. You're doing your best to make the right decisions and to put the right strategies in place, but major events personally or professionally are throwing you off kilter. These can include:

- *Personal*
  - Illness or injury

- New child or other transitions involving kids
- Start or end of a relationship
- Move or natural disaster
- *Professional*
  - New business
  - Product launch
  - Busy holiday season
  - Change of job responsibilities

In these seasons:

- **Give yourself grace**—If you're in the midst of a major personal or professional change, you will feel more pressure and may have a hard time keeping on top of things that usually come naturally to you. That's okay. It's fine to lower your expectations in certain areas, and it's essential to take time to refresh and rejuvenate during these times instead of pushing yourself into a frenzy.
- **Avoid creating drama**—Some phases of life are unavoidable, but often we create our own craziness. If you're a business owner, you can typically set the pace of how quickly you move forward on developing your business or how many contracts you take on at a time. To keep your sanity, it's essential that you know what's on your plate and say, "No," when necessary. Also, it's a good idea to avoid major business changes when you know that you have major personal commitments coming up. Even as an employee, you can typically take leave, set boundaries, or find a new job to decrease the drama.
- **Be honest**—If a "phase" extends out over months or even years, you're probably facing a major systemic decision or a situational strategy problem. Seriously think through what responsibility you have to make macro- or micro-level changes.
- **Rest and recover**—At the end of a really busy season in your life, you need time to rest and recover. Not only is this a nice idea, but it's also absolutely necessary to give you time to heal and come back strong. I don't recommend giving yourself an indefinite rest period because you may lose too much momentum and, in turn, confidence. But I do encourage you to set

aside a certain amount of time to slow down the pace, sort through some of your backlog, and decide how you want to move forward with your life and work.

DO YOU THRIVE IN YOUR WORK ENVIRONMENT?

Most adults spend most of their time in a working environment, whether in a traditional job, running their own business, or caring for children or family members. Every work ecosystem has intrinsic qualities most often called *culture*, much like every biological ecosystem has different attributes usually referred to as the *habitat*. Certain plants and animals thrive in certain habitats. For instance, a palm tree would freeze in a snap in Antarctica, whereas most penguins would overheat in Hawaii. Plants and animals survive and thrive when in their proper zones.

In the same way, you need the right work environment to be your best self and do your best work. Signs that you may need a change of environment include

- Dreading going into the office
- Feeling alone and like an outsider
- Needing to defend your priorities on a continual basis
- Decreasing confidence
- Fearing interaction with your boss
- Fighting back frustration at the way things get done
- Receiving criticism for attempts to improve your work
- Hiding your true personality and strengths to fit in

If you can't thrive in your current work environment, even after taking steps to better the situation, it's usually a sign that you need to make a major systemic decision, as noted earlier under "Balancing and Rebalancing." Staying true to your priorities is hard enough without having to constantly fight against critics. Here's how Brett Sonnenschein, husband of the editorial director of *Working Mother*,[5] described how he kept himself in a working environment where he could stay aligned with his personal definition of success:

When our daughter, Gwendolyn, was born in 2003, I negotiated to leave work twice a week at 5 p.m. to pick her up from childcare. A few years in, a new boss arrived who seemed desperate to break that deal but couldn't do it outright. Instead, he lectured me that work was more important than family because "work supports our family." He extolled his last job, where he'd go on the road for two weeks or more, leaving his working wife to take care of the kids on her own. Seeing where this was leading, I kept my mouth shut and in a few months found another job where flexibility ruled.

These days, the biggest change I've experienced as a working father has been how I define success. Equally important as salary and meaningful work is the ability to race out twice a week at 5 p.m. to pick up two kids who, more often than not, run at me with dueling play-date requests, gripping artwork thick with paint that will never dry. Of course, it's usually right at that moment that my cell phone will ring with a work call (or the latest Mets score—come on, I'm only human!). Just being able to pull it all off defines success for me.

Do you see how Brett made the choice to move to a more hospitable ecosystem? I know that this shift isn't always possible, but when you can, seek out companies and managers who will work with you, not against you. This could include giving you the freedom to leave early to pick up your kids or supporting you in working extra hard so that you can build a new international division. The point isn't that you should work more or less, but that you should find a place where you feel accepted, supported, and rewarded for investing your time in alignment with your priorities and how you work best.

. . . .
Journaling Exercise: Go Take a Nap!

So we've discovered Secret #1: Clarify Action-Based Priorities and gone through how you can define your personal definition of success and use it to make decisions and keep your time investment consistently aligned with your priorities.

But as we conclude this chapter, we must return to a lesson you learned in kindergarten but probably thought you outgrew: If you don't sleep, you get grumpy. Despite popular opinion, Maslow's hierarchy of needs applies at any age, and basic self-care, such as sleeping well and eating well, plays a foundational role in achieving more success with less stress. Here's my story of how I relearned to make sleep a priority:

> It all started in high school when I would fall asleep on the dining room floor wrapped up in a blanket and struggling to finish my U.S. history reading. Then it continued on to college, my corporate career, and finally into my business. No matter how much I said that I wanted to get enough sleep, I just never seemed to be able to go to bed early enough and/or sleep in late enough to make it happen.
>
> I was chronically sleep-deprived.
>
> Fortunately, I heard a message a few years ago that changed my attitude on sleep. The speaker's point was simple but profound: "Don't say, 'When,' say 'How?'"
>
> With so many important things in life from paying down debt to spending time with people to getting enough sleep, we tell ourselves:
>
> - When I get a new job . . .
> - When this project is over . . .
> - When my kids grow up . . .
> - When my business is really growing . . .
>
> then I'll . . .
>
> - take care of myself.
> - slow down.
> - exercise and eat right.
> - etc., etc., etc.

It's true that we have certain intense times in our life, such as when we have a new baby, move, put on a huge event, or must meet a project deadline. But if we're always saying, "When," and never moving forward on our life goals, it's time to start asking, "How can I do this now?"

For instance, with sleep, I realized that I just needed to start making it a priority. I do best with about seven hours of sleep, preferably from 11 p.m. to 6 a.m. Depriving my body of this basic need wasn't something I should perpetually put off until "life was more calm."

To make this happen, I first had to realize that this was a "How can I do this now?" activity. Then I had to think through what kept me from following this routine. I recognized a couple of ways I kept myself from getting enough sleep:

- Starting to get ready around 11 p.m.

- Staying out late at events

- Working on projects at the last minute

- Being unrealistic about how much I could get done in an evening

- Watching movies or checking e-mail late at night

Once I realized that I was choosing to do these activities that were keeping me from my goal of seven hours of sleep and that I needed to and could make sleep a priority, I decided to take a proactive approach by:

- Telling myself that I needed to get ready around 10 p.m. so that my brain could start to wind down and my teeth would be brushed and faced washed before 11 p.m.

- Deciding before I went to an event when I wanted to leave and, if I was carpooling with someone, asking that person in advance if we could head out at a certain time.

- Giving myself a personal deadline that was the day before the actual client deadline. In this way, if projects took longer than expected, I didn't have to stay up until midnight.

- Thinking through how long it would take me to do each of the activities I hoped to accomplish on a particu-

lar evening and then evaluating that versus how many hours I actually had to spend before emotionally committing to getting a long list of things done before I went to bed.

- Planning a cutoff time of 10 p.m. to turn off my computer or the TV so that I wasn't tempted to keep connected and my mind would have a chance to wind down.

I can't say that every single night I'm asleep by 11:01 p.m. But what I can say is that in general I do get about seven hours of sleep and that it doesn't tend to be a major struggle to get up in the morning. Also, I am

- More alert during the day (I used to practically fall asleep at my desk between 2 and 3 p.m.)

- Less likely to get sick (I rarely get sick, and if I do, I usually get well quickly.)

- More engaged and present when I interact with people

- More calm when faced with stress or strain

Journaling Questions

Now over to you. . . . How is your sleep schedule? Consider these questions:

- When was a time I have felt most rested?

- How many hours of sleep leave me feeling satisfied?

- When do I get up both during the weekdays and on weekends?

- When would I like to get up? Why?

- Are there certain activities that I would like to do in the morning before I start work? If so, what are they?

- When would I need to get up to make those happen?

- When do I naturally start to get tired in the evening?

- When do I need to go to bed in order to get the number of hours of sleep that I need?

- When would I need to get home at night or start winding down to make that happen?

Once, you've decided when you would like to get up, go to bed, and get ready for bed, it's important to decide why this is so important. Some of your "whys" could be:

- Better health
- Increased energy
- Improved mood
- Opportunity to exercise
- Less rush-hour traffic
- Meditation time

When you're tempted to fall back into your old habits of sleep deprivation, think back to why sleep is so important to you, and think through "how" to make it happen. Here are some questions to ask yourself:

- What activities or habits are keeping me up late?

- What's keeping me from getting up in the morning?

Then here are some tips to try:

- Set a timer about an hour or two before you actually have to go to sleep to prompt you to start getting ready for bed.
- Ask your spouse or roommate to keep you accountable to turn off the computer or TV at a certain time or install an automatic shut-off program.

- Schedule activities early in the morning, such as walking with a friend or doing conference calls, which will force you to get up.

- Plan in exercise to increase your energy during the day and your fatigue at night.

- Transition your children to an earlier sleep schedule so that you can have more free time after they go to bed and so that they can get the sleep they need to be alert at school.

Also, if you are struggling with severe fatigue, even when you are getting a large amount of sleep, see your doctor. You might need help with exercise, nutrition, or other health concerns, such as low thyroid levels or sleep apnea. Your health is important, and setting when you want to get up and go to bed is a key first step in effective time investment.

You have the opportunity to live a life aligned with your priorities starting now! Embrace the opportunity!

. . . .

Notes

1. Gretchen Rubin, "Do You Fall into This Happiness Trap? The False Choice." The Happiness Project. Available at: http://happiness-project.com/happiness_project/2012/05/do-you-fall-into-this-happiness-trap-the-false-choice.

2. Eric Farkas, "How To Do a Startup on the Side and Not Lose Your Family," *Hacker News*. Available at: http://ericfarkas.com/posts/how-to-do-a-startup-on-the-side-and-not-lose-your-family.

3. Jessica Stillman, "Why Working More than 40 Hours a Week Is Useless," *Inc.* Available at: http://www.inc.com/jessica-stillman/why-working-more-than-40-hours-a-week-is-useless.html.

4. Bethenny Frankel, *A Place of Yes: 10 Rules for Getting Everything You Want Out of Life*. New York: Touchstone, 2011.

5. Brett Sonnenschein, *Working Mother*, June–July 2012, p. 6.

CHAPTER 5

SECRET #2

Set Realistic Expectations

*I don't know the key to success, but the key to failure
is trying to please everybody.*

—BILL COSBY, ACTOR AND COMEDIAN

A Tale of Two Expectations

TABLE 5.1 *Realistic Daily Expectations*

THE SITUATION	REALISTIC EXPECTATIONS	NOT-SO-REALISTIC EXPECTATIONS
Getting up	I know that I like to hit "Snooze" a couple of times each morning. So that I'm not rushed and still have time to enjoy my coffee, I'll set my alarm for an hour before I need to walk out the door. I'll also pack my lunch, wash the dishes in the sink, and lay out my clothes the night before because these activities cause me stress in the morning.	I set my alarm for 20 minutes before I need to leave the house so that I should have exactly enough time to grab coffee, get dressed, pack my lunch, and leave. *Why am I so stressed in the morning, running late all the time, and always needing to buy a lunch? Oh yeah, and the house is a mess.*

(continued)

TABLE 5.1 *Realistic Daily Expectations* (continued)

THE SITUATION	REALISTIC EXPECTATIONS	NOT-SO-REALISTIC EXPECTATIONS
Commute	I know that it technically only takes a little over an hour for me to get to work. But when I have an 8 a.m. meeting and it's really essential that I make it to work exactly on time, I give myself one and a half hours. That way, if I'm running a bit late, I hit some traffic, it's raining, or something else comes up to slow me down, I'm not stressed. I know I'll be at work on time, and if everything goes smoothly, I can even knock something off my to-do list.	If I hit every green light, find a close parking spot, and don't have people in front of me in line, it takes 11 minutes for me to get to the train station, park, buy a ticket, and board the train. Then, once I get off the 41-minute train ride, if I walk really quickly and don't have to wait for the elevator, it takes me 13 minutes to get from the train to my office. I'll leave the house at 6:55 a.m. when I have an 8 a.m. meeting. *Shoot! I'm late again. What's wrong with me?!*
Planning and processing	I know that planning plays an essential role in my feeling in control and on top of my daily activities and in being proactive about my big goals. I set aside time at the start of each day to review my calendar and my to-do list and to set priorities. I also anticipate anything that might come up in the next couple of days and proactively take action to avoid potential problems. Each day, I also set aside a focused amount of time to respond to all of my new e-mails and to record any corresponding tasks that I need to do in relation to the e-mails. That way I'm on top of what's in my inbox, and I can focus on executing on projects the rest of the day.	I've got so much to do that I couldn't possibly waste time on such activities as answering my e-mails or planning. I'll just plunge into the first activity that captures my attention and work as hard as I can. Then, when I have a few minutes between meetings, on the train, or after dinner, I'll catch up on e-mails. *I hate that I'm always afraid I will forget something and that I'm always getting things done at the last minute. My anxiety rises with my ever-growing e-mail inbox, and sometimes I even forget about meetings . . . that's so embarrassing. Why can't I feel like I have it together?*

THE SITUATION	REALISTIC EXPECTATIONS	NOT-SO-REALISTIC EXPECTATIONS
Getting tasks done	I carefully map out when I will work on certain activities throughout my week to ensure that I have enough time for what's most important. If I have a deadline, I make a personal deadline a day or two before the actual one so that I have some wiggle room in case of unexpected technical problems or meetings that run long. When people ask me to do something new, I evaluate whether I have time to help them now. If I don't, I let them know who else could assist them immediately, or I tell them when I will have the ability to assist them.	I've always been a "can do" type of person, so I figure if I throw myself hard enough at tasks, anything is possible. I also really like to help other people, so if anyone has a question at any time, I try to help them immediately. I'm more or less the go-to person for everything. *Why do I feel like I never have enough time to get things done and like I'm taking care of everyone else's priorities but not my own?*
Wrapping up	I set up a pop-up alarm on my computer for one hour before I want to leave to remind myself to start wrapping up my current tasks. I also avoid scheduling any meetings for the last hour of the day or starting on any completely new tasks. I assess and review how the day went, adding any new action items to my to-do list. I do a quick scan of my e-mails to make sure that nothing urgent has come up, and I also listen and, if necessary, respond to my voicemails. I start to save and to close down the different documents on my computer and then look around my desk to see if I need to toss or file anything. I also do a quick mental check to make sure that I have everything I need to bring home with me before I step away from my desk.	The end of the day always catches me off guard. Usually what happens is that I glance at the clock on my computer and realize that it's 6:30 p.m., and if I don't leave soon, I'm going to need to wait a long time for the next train. I quickly save my documents (but still leave them open), grab my coat, and run for the station. *Why do I always feel like I need to check my e-mail at night to make sure that something important hasn't come up? Why is my office a disaster? Why do I always feel like I have a bunch of unfinished work that I need to sort out in the morning? Oh . . . and it's so irritating when I leave something at the office, such as my phone or keys, or I miss the train and need to eat dinner really late.*

(continued)

TABLE 5.1 *Realistic Daily Expectations (continued)*

THE SITUATION	REALISTIC EXPECTATIONS	NOT-SO-REALISTIC EXPECTATIONS
Dinner	I like to occasionally splurge on a nice dinner out, but usually I cook dinner at home either for just myself or for a small group of friends. To make grocery shopping easier, I keep a running list on my phone that includes the basics, such as toilet paper, milk, and bread, and then I add to it throughout the week when I run out of something. Before I head to the grocery store, I take a quick look through my cupboards to see what I have and then sketch out a rough meal plan for the week, making sure that I have fruits, vegetables, protein sources, and starches. On a daily basis, I make something simple according to my mood and try to cook a little extra so that I have enough for leftovers.	I spend hours on the weekend salivating over four-course meals that magically appear before my eyes on the Food Network and savoring recipes on organic-food-cooking blogs. I know exactly which superfoods I should eat, such as wheatgrass and bee pollen, and how to make dairy-free, gluten-free anything. But knowing so much makes me very particular, so I don't want to grocery shop unless I can go to Whole Foods. Also, I feel overwhelmed by the thought of just whipping something up because it might not have just the right combination of essential nutrients and nuanced flavors. *Why do I end up ordering pizza more nights than I would like to admit while the meager ingredients I do have in my fridge grow mold?*
Exercise	I try to go on a walk twice a week during lunch with one of my coworkers. It's a nice chance for us to catch up, get outside, and reenergize for the afternoon. I have some Pilates and yoga workout DVDs, so I try to do those a couple of nights during the week and once on the weekend. I enjoy dancing, so that's also something I do about once or twice a month for some fun and some great aerobic exercise. I'm no triathlete, but I feel healthy, energized, and pain-free most of the time.	I haven't done any exercise in the past year, but I would really like to train for a marathon. I admire people in great shape, and running clubs seem like a good bonding experience. I am going to get started as soon as I buy the perfect running outfit, find a running club in my area, contact its organizer, see if its practice times fit with my schedule, sign up, figure out how I can best get to and from the club meetings, and know that I can really stick with a consistent running schedule. *Why can I never find time to exercise? I feel like I'm getting so out of shape!*

THE SITUATION	REALISTIC EXPECTATIONS	NOT-SO-REALISTIC EXPECTATIONS
Evening plans	On nights when I have some sort of event, I can really only eat dinner, clean up after dinner, do a bit of exercise, and check e-mail quickly before heading to bed. On evenings when I don't have a planned activity, I can usually get one or two other items done after work, such as going to the grocery store or making some progress on a home project, but not much else.	On the way home from work, I always make a mental checklist of all I will accomplish in an evening: three loads of laundry, cleaning the bathroom, sorting the mail, cooking something from scratch, sending a thoughtful reply to a friend's e-mail, hanging up my clothes, watching my favorite TV show, calling my mom, and reading a chapter of a new book. *Why do I always end up sitting on the coach and doing nothing because I'm completely overwhelmed?*
Sleep	I know how much sleep I need to be my best self, so I make it a priority to leave events early enough for my brain to calm down before I go to bed. Once I'm home, I start shutting down my computer, TV set, and other electronic items at least a half an hour before bedtime. Then I go through each room, shutting off overhead lights, straightening anything out of place, and generally reassuring myself that all will be well until the next morning. After that, I brush my teeth, wash my face, change into my pajamas, and get myself into bed so that I can turn out the lights at a reasonable hour.	When I'm out at events, I don't notice the time until everyone starts to leave, and I realize that—once again—I've stayed out too late. When I've spent the evening at home and the 10 o'clock news flashes on the screen, I go into a bit of a panic. That's the point where I realize that I just spent the last few hours watching television and got nothing done that I meant to do. Instead of starting to wind down for the night, I frantically attempt to check some items off of my to-do list so that I feel like I "deserve" to go to sleep. This late-night burst of productivity often leads to a half-cleaned kitchen and laundry sitting in the washer overnight so that it has a bit of a dank smell in the morning. I then drop into bed a few hours past my bedtime, but I often can't fall asleep because my mind still buzzes from the late-night surge of activity. *Why do I feel so tired all the time, and why do I struggle sooooo much to get up in the morning?*

Do you get the picture of how expectations can make a *huge* difference in both the big priorities and the small details of life? The bottom-line answer to every question in the right-hand column is this: You don't have realistic expectations. If any of those scenarios sounded uncomfortably familiar, I have good news for you: Shifting your expectations from the right-hand column to the middle column can dramatically transform your experience of life and empower you to achieve more success with less stress.

Secret #2: Set Realistic Expectations

Here's the truth: Reality always wins. You can either fight it or join it. But you will only feel good about what you achieve in a day when you embrace the reality of your situation. This is why Secret #2 is *set realistic expectations*. Let's break down the three parts:

Set: *To adjust to a desired position.* As with priorities, if you don't set expectations of yourself, others will happily set them for you. But when you embrace the possible in your situation and accept your capacity, you put yourself in a position to truly feel successful. I know that this may seem horribly un-motivational-speaker-like, but I need you to trust me on this point. As you saw in Table 5.1, you actually achieve more when you set reasonable standards. When you do big-picture dreaming about priorities, shoot for the seemingly impossible. But when you set day-to-day expectations on progressing toward your goals, aim at the possible.

Realistic: *Tending to or expressing an awareness of things as they really are.* In the realm of effective time investment, being *realistic* involves taking traditional cerebral time-management tools such as to-do lists and priorities and marrying them with a down-to-earth understanding of the finite nature of time and the fluctuating nature of life. For example, some people dismiss the idea of weekly planning because things rarely go exactly according to plan. True. To assume that they would is unrealistic. However, we can adjust our expectations to be: By making to-do lists and by

overlaying them over our calendars, we can consistently complete the most important activities, remember all the details, and proactively work ahead with the full knowledge that some of the less important and urgent items will slide to the next week, and that's okay. If you think of your weekly plan like taking a canoe trip, it's not hitting every stopping point at a specific time that matters but arriving each evening at your campsite before nightfall and returning home by the end of the week.

Expectations: *Strong beliefs that something will happen or be the case in the future.* We don't evaluate certain results as success or failure based on their intrinsic qualities but rather on our expectations of what could or should happen. For example, suppose that a project takes you eight hours to complete. If your expectation was that it would take six hours, you're frustrated; that it would take eight hours, you're content; and that it would take 10 hours, you're ecstatic! Another example: You finish a half-marathon in two hours and 10 minutes. If your expectation was that you didn't think you would finish, you're extremely happy; that you would run around that time, you're satisfied; or that you would win the race, you're disappointed in yourself. In both examples, the reality of what happened did not change, but your expectations dramatically affected your interpretation of the results. This is why you want to set realistic expectations—so that you set yourself up to feel motivated and accomplished.

TABLE 5.2 *Key Mental Shift: Realistic Expectations*

HARMFUL	HELPFUL
It will be different next time.	Unless my actions or something about the situation changes, the results next time will be exactly the same as before.
I don't want to know the truth. It's too intimidating.	When I'm in touch with reality, I put myself in the best position to be proactive and successful.

Expectations of Yourself:
Let Go of Comparison and Perfectionism

The most important, yet often the most difficult, step in implementing Secret #2 is setting realistic expectations of yourself. This requires first daring to dream that you don't need to live a time-poor life and then choosing to take responsibility for setting and meeting realistic expectations.

> ▶ **RED FLAGS:** Some people purposely avoid setting realistic expectations for themselves because then they always have an excuse for not following through and keeping their word. If this sounds like you, I encourage you to take the more responsible approach of starting to make and keep realistic commitments.

The two biggest areas where I see people fall into unrealistic expectations of themselves in regard to time investment are comparison and perfectionism. Let's examine how you can develop the proper mind-set and then choose to act differently.

Comparison: Why Can't I Be Like _____?
I love personality tests like those mentioned in Chapter 1 because they not only help you to better understand yourself but also give you an appreciation for others' unique perspective and strengths. If you've never looked into the Myers-Briggs Type Indicator, the Riso-Hudson Enneagram Type Indicator, or the StrengthsFinder, I encourage you to check them out. These tests will help you to understand that finding some things extremely difficult, such as focusing on one task or setting priorities, does not mean that you're a bad person or that something is wrong with you. It simply means that these capacities don't fall within your natural strengths, and you need to consciously work on increasing your capabilities in these areas. I've noticed that people also can judge themselves negatively based on the following sorts of differences that have nothing to do with right or wrong, good or bad. We need to accept who we are and let go of comparison so that we can begin to learn how to invest our time most effectively:

- **Moderators versus abstainers.** As discussed in Chapter 1, moderators are the type of people who do best when they check social media for 10 minutes three times a day. Abstainers know that they can't get on Facebook without being distracted for an hour. Embrace that you are a moderator or an abstainer, and set your expectations accordingly.
- **Energy levels.** To a certain degree, we can increase our energy levels through proper self-care, such as sleep, eating, and exercise, and keeping ourselves in an emotionally positive state. Even when two people reach their peak energy state, though, the results may look very different. One may need only four hours of sleep, whereas the other may need eight. One may be able to focus for only an hour at a time, whereas the other may have the capacity to sink into a project for four hours straight. Pay attention to what you really need to be your best, and don't worry if that varies from what others need. For some extra insight into your intensity and length of response to situations, check out whether your temperament falls within the choleric, melancholic, sanguine, or phlegmatic range.
- **Thinking styles.** According to Dr. Kathy Benzinger,[1] people have natural strengths in a certain quadrant of their brain. To help individuals understand how to identify their natural strengths and how to find a profession and a work environment that allows them to thrive, she developed the Benzinger Thinking Styles Assessment and wrote *Thriving in Mind*. This research helps you to understand how falsifying your type can lead to fatigue and ineffectiveness, whereas working with it allows you to unleash your brilliance.
- **Outside variables.** So many factors play a role in what different people can accomplish. If it seems like someone has superhuman capabilities, it may come as a result of having an incredibly supportive significant other or the financial means to hire out house cleaning and grocery shopping or a super short commute or any number of other advantages that you may or may not have. Instead of beating yourself up about your performance, ask the person how he or she manages so well (you might learn some fantastic strategies). Also keep in mind that you may not know about some of the struggles that the person faces or sacrifices that he or she makes.

TABLE 5.3 *Key Mental Shift: Comparison*

HARMFUL	HELPFUL
I must be as good as or better than everyone around me.	I can accept myself as I am right now and celebrate improvement from my previous performance.

Self-Compassion: The Antidote to Comparison

The common mentality that you should push yourself relentlessly to measure up may produce counterproductive results. *The New York Times* article, "Go Easy on Yourself, a New Wave of Research Shows,"[2] explains how many people who can act quite understanding and supportive of others tend to beat themselves up for not behaving perfectly:

> *The research suggests that giving ourselves a break and accepting our imperfections may be the first step toward better health. People who score high on tests of self-compassion have less depression and anxiety, and tend to be happier and more optimistic. Preliminary data suggest that self-compassion can even influence how much we eat and may help some people lose weight.*

To increase your self-compassion talk to yourself in this manner:

- **Accept yourself as you are.** "Even though I _____, I deeply and completely accept myself."
- **Validate the difficulty of the challenge.** "Everyone makes mistakes sometimes. I'm making a difficult change, and it's okay if I encounter some setbacks along the way."
- **Celebrate progress in relation to your past performance.** "I'm no Mozart, but I just played 'Twinkle, Twinkle Little Star' more smoothly than I did last week."

For more information on how to practice self-compassion, you can check out Dr. Kristin Neff's book, *Self-Compassion: Stop Beating Yourself Up and Leave Insecurity Behind*, or go to www.self-compassion.org to assess your level of self-compassion and find more resources.

TABLE 5.4 *Expectations Shifters*

WARNING: EXPECTATIONS SHIFTS AHEAD	
SHORT PERSONAL DETOURS (REQUIRE SLIGHT SHIFTS IN EXPECTATIONS)	**MAJOR LIFE CONSTRUCTION (REQUIRES MAJOR SHIFTS IN EXPECTATIONS)**
Project deadline	Moving to a new location
Sick with a cold	Significant illness
Unexpected meetings	Having a child
Bad traffic	Getting married
Last-minute client request	Starting a serious relationship
Computer glitch	Ending a relationship
Bad night of sleep	New job or business
Increased job responsibilities	Losing a job or client
Car troubles	Death of a loved one
Home appliance stops working	Child leaving home
Friends or family needing help	Financial troubles

Perfectionism: Less Than Ideal Is Failure

Perfectionism manifests on the surface in two very different forms: perfectionists and frustrated perfectionists. The first form leads to a sort of pandemonium, where you attempt to do everything all at once not only for yourself but also for all those around you. You live in a constant state of attention, scrutinizing yourself and others for any sign of a "crack" in the facade. Every time you spot one, you scurry to quickly cover up the evidence that you can't truly meet your impossible standards. In the second form, this mind-set leads to paralysis. Frustrated perfectionists may seem lazy on the surface, but their minds work on overdrive. They imagine and reimagine and rethink and recontemplate how they might do something in the most ideal fashion and achieve the most superior result. Given the grandiosity of their vision, though, they feel like they're doomed to fail prior to beginning. As one of my time coaching clients said to me, "I've got everything so perfectly imagined in my head that I know I can never live up to my standard." Such people usually do not start anything at all or wait until the last minute. This delays them from having to face up to the raw truth that they can't meet their own unrealistic ideals and allows them to blame their lack of time for lack of results.

Despite the diametrically opposite appearances on the surface, though, the same deep-seated fears lie below: "Doing anything imperfectly not only leads to unacceptable results but also means that I'm unacceptable. Everything I do or don't do has an impact on my personal value and self-worth."

This toxic mind-set makes effective time investment really, really difficult because you have a huge emotional connection to your productivity—or lack thereof. Since you most likely developed this mind-set at a young age, it's hard for you to imagine that you could think in any other way. To retrain your mind to believe that you can safely let go of the expectation of perfection, you'll need to focus on these two areas:

- **Change your thoughts.** The root causes behind perfectionism typically lie in the crippling emotions of guilt, fear, or shame. Go back to Chapter 2 and review how you can let go of these "joy stealers," and then revisit Chapter 3 to come up with new, empowering affirmations. At first, this will seem wholly unnatural and potentially even harmful. You may think, "I'm already inadequate. Won't relaxing my standards lead to disaster?" But, as explained earlier, self-compassion can free you to accomplish more. Ninety percent perfect and done almost always leads to a bigger positive impact than 100 percent perfect and stuck in your head. If you find yourself continuing to struggle with the idea of letting go of impossible standards for yourself, gently nudge your conscience with these sorts of questions:
  - What really matters most to me?
  - Is perfectionism helping me to achieve what's most important or holding me back?
  - What would happen if I relaxed my standards? Would the world really come to an end?
  - Finally, my favorite, from a human resources executive at a major airline: Is there blood? She always asks her staff this question when they start to get stressed out to help them put the situation into perspective.
- **Distance your critics.** If you grew up in a family where you would get a 99 percent on a test and your parents would ask you what happened to the other 1 percent, then you're probably used to the people around

you reinforcing your perfectionist tendencies. During the process of retraining your mind, observe which situations or people trigger your perfectionism or feeling of inadequacy: Do you consistently put yourself into unstable environments where you're driven to obsession to maintain some sense of control? Do you agree with your critics who tell you that you're worthless, useless, and less than other higher achievers? If you answered "Yes" to either one of these questions, you'll need to work on limiting the time you spend in these environments so that you have the ability to rebuild new helpful mental patterns. You also can practice filtering inputs before accepting them into your psyche. What this means is that when someone says something to you that could snap you into perfectionist defensiveness, you stop to take a moment to question the input. You can ask yourself: Is this true? Did I actually do something wrong? Do I choose to accept this statement about me or my work? This conscious reflection gives you the power to deflect harmful ideas before they take root in your mind.

TABLE 5.5 *Key Mental Shift: Perfectionism*

HARMFUL	HELPFUL
Less than perfect is failure and a disaster.	I don't need to fear results. I can only choose to do my best and use every experience to learn how to do better in the future.

▶ **RED FLAGS FOR PERFECTIONISM:** Often feeling tired (but compelled to keep going), lonely (even when around people), and like a failure (even when receiving accolades).

INO Technique: A Practical Approach to Perfect Time Allocation

Once you adopt the healthy perspective that you don't need to expect perfection from yourself, you need to change your prior habit of approaching everything as something that must be done perfectly. In my experience as a time coach, I've found that simply telling recovering perfectionists to calm down and not take everything so seriously doesn't work very well for two reasons:

- Sometimes striving for close to perfection really does matter, such as when you perform a surgery or when you work on an extremely important project where small details can make a significant difference.
- People with perfectionist tendencies often get a really great sense of satisfaction in doing something really well, whether it's throwing a party or coding a website. To deprive yourself of ever doing anything to a high standard would leave you entirely dissatisfied.

In response to these two factors, I've developed the *INO technique*. This method allows you to discern how you should approach your time investments in different types of activities instead of approaching everything from a place of perfection. What you'll want to do as you're planning your day and then starting in on an activity is to ask yourself which category best describes this activity and then to invest your time accordingly:

- **Investment activities.** These activities can produce a higher rate of return when you invest more time in them. When it comes to your most important personal priorities, such as spending time with the people who matter most to you, and professional priorities, such as business-development strategies, maximize the amount of time that you invest in these items.
- **Neutral activities.** These to-do items produce a return in direct correlation with the amount of time that you put into them. An example on the personal side could be exercising or on the work side could be basic project management or hourly contract work. You don't need to minimize the time you spend in these areas, but you also don't need to maximize it. Look to contain your time investment in these items so that you can move on to investment activities as soon as possible.
- **Optimize activities.** These tasks produce no greater value when you invest more time in them, so the faster they get done, the better. On the home front, this could mean maintenance work around your house, and on the work front, it could mean answering e-mails. If you can have other people do these activities for you, delegate them. If you need to do them yourself, challenge yourself to complete them in the shortest possible amount of time.

As an added bonus, I thought I would share the following assessment that I went through with one of my clients to help him objectively evaluate his perfectionist tendencies. The point of the exercise was to go from always aiming for perfection to practicing the INO technique so that he could spend a whole lot less effort on such items as ordering office supplies and focus more on high-value time investments such as his graphic design projects.

Deciding When to Aim for "Perfect"

Areas Where You Tend to Aim for Perfection

- **Design.** Want to wow people with your work
  - **Why?** You like the affirmation, want to receive more work you enjoy, and you're an artist who takes pleasure in the process.
- **Ordering.** Want the best, most efficient solution at the lowest cost
  - **Why?** It gives you satisfaction to know that you're helping people save time and do their work better and that you're saving the company money.
- **Communication.** Want e-mails, product forms, and other company documents to look good and be error-free
  - **Why?** You don't like making errors. You feel like a flaw destroys the credibility of the whole piece. You tend to make things new and custom instead of using templates.

What's the Cost of Wanting Everything to Be Perfect?

- Stay later.
- Work longer hours with fewer breaks.
- Push back work on other projects.
- For each perfect completion, you feel like you create two problems because you neglected other activities.
- Values conflict with other marketing person, who wants everything quickly and doesn't care if it's "fancy."
- Boss has to give you multiple reminders to finish an activity.

When Is Perfection Worth the Cost of Extra Time?

- When you're working on a project you really care about, when the project aligns with your goals, and when it can go in your portfolio.
- When you can do something that really pleases the president of the company, such as making scientific figures look beautiful.
- When a particular purchase will lead to a significant time and cost savings for people who are producing high-value work.

When Is Perfection Not Worth the Cost?

- When something is easy to go back and change later if you have extra time and energy: blog posts, some posters. (You can put these items on your low-priority to-do list.)
- When you're ordering items with relatively small variance in price and utility, such as paper clips and staplers.
- When small changes to a template could sufficiently communicate to your clients instead of a complete custom rewrite and redesign of a form.

Some Mental Reminders

- It's good for me to desire the company to look professional and for people to trust the quality of my work and my integrity, but I don't need to be afraid of making any mistake.
- By focusing my perfectionist tendency on what really matters and limiting my time on other activities, I can retain my "awesome designer" brand and get projects done on time. People will be able to rely on me and trust me even more.
- If I turn things in late, people are frustrated, but they won't give me less to do, so it's not a good strategy for reducing my workload!
- With many things, minor errors won't have a major impact.
- I don't need to be afraid of upsetting people. If I need to do something that isn't what someone would prefer, I can go to him or her and explain the situation.

- I can decide that something is good enough and let it go so that I have time for what's most important and to relax. I can give myself "closure" before I've achieved perfection.
- Trying to make everyone else happy 100 percent of the time will lead to me being happy 0 percent of the time. I can choose to make self-care and energizing activities a priority. I'm worth it.

By letting go of perfectionism, you can get more done, invest the most time in what matters most, and feel like a success.

Others' Expectations of You: Let Go of Pressure and Guilt

When other people have unrealistic expectations of us, either it can drive us to push harder and harder in a desperate attempt to one day win their approval or it can swing us in the opposite direction of defiance, resentment, or hiding. Fortunately, you have the ability to modify people's expectations of your behavior whether they generated the expectations themselves or you taught them to have unrealistic expectations.

Pressure: When Others Put Unrealistic Expectations on You
Others can put unrealistic expectations on you when they don't recognize your distinct differences, as we discussed in the section on avoiding comparison. In those situations, you can learn more about your personality type and explain to them why certain activities pose greater difficulties for you than for them. In other instances, they are unaware of how much you have going on right now and/or how long it will take for you to do what they have requested that you do. I've found that these sorts of expectations frustrations happen quite often between clients and small-business owners and between bosses and employees.

TABLE 5.6 *Key Mental Shift: Pressure*

HARMFUL	HELPFUL
It's impossible for me to meet these expectations, but I just need to suck it up and deal with it.	I need to get a clear sense of what's on my agenda right now and then talk through what's reasonable with the other people involved.

Expectations Negotiation: Setting the Stage
for an Informed Discussion

If you happen to be the pressured small-business owner or employee, you can help your client or boss understand what is realistic by following these four steps:

- **Step 1**: Document in detail all of the projects you have going on right now, including the main deadlines and deliverables.
- **Step 2**: Estimate how long each portion of the project should take.
- **Step 3**: Overlay these estimates over your work hours, remembering that not all your hours will be devoted to this project. (You will need to dedicate some time to meetings, e-mail, other projects, etc.)
- **Step 4**: Talk through your findings with your boss or client.

The conversation may sound something like this:

Your Initial E-mail

Hi Bill,

I'd like to have a conversation with you about the projects that I'm working on right now. That way, we can both be on the same page about what's most important and what deadlines seem reasonable. Does that sound good to you?

    If so, I'm free on Monday at 2 p.m. or Wednesday at 11 a.m. What time and meeting place would work best for you?

All the best,

Proactive Employee

Your Meeting Dialogue

You: *Hi Bill! Thanks for taking the time to meet with me. I really appreciate it.*
Bill: *Not a problem. What would you like to talk about?*

You: *Well, I took some time to evaluate the projects that I'm working on for you and to break down my estimates for each portion.*

Bill: *Okay, that sounds good.*

You: *Yes, it was really good and helped me to get a handle on the scope of what we're working on right now. Here's a list of the key deliverables and our current milestones. [Slide list over to Bill on cue.]*

Bill: *Wow. It seems like we've got quite a lot going on right now.*

You: *Yes, we do. And when I overlaid the estimates over my current schedule, the numbers didn't match up.*

- **Tactic #1:** This got a deadline extension for one of my time coaching clients who had a 30-hour-per-week contract for information technology work and had previously just put in extra unpaid hours to try to meet his client's unrealistic expectations.

    You: *Since I'm contracted with you to do 30 hours of work a week, it won't be possible for me to complete the projects by the initial deadlines you set. Would it be reasonable for me to have another two weeks to complete the first project and an additional five days on the second one?*

- **Tactic #2:** This helped one of my time coaching clients who serves many teams in his corporation to clarify how to align his priorities with his boss's priorities and to know where he could ask people to lower their expectations of his involvement.

    You: *Given that I only have a limited amount of time each week to move these projects forward, where would you like me to focus? I want to make sure that I'm investing the most time in the items that you consider a high priority. Also, if I need to let some teams know that I can't provide as much support to them right now, I want to know that you feel comfortable backing that decision. What are your thoughts?*

These approaches tend to work very well because they take the conversation from simply saying you feel overwhelmed to talking through

tangible facts in terms of the scope of the work and the time investment involved. This allows you to work together as a team to problem-solve and decide on expectations based in reality.

DELOITTE CASE STUDY: MASS CAREER CUSTOMIZATION

The method that I described for reducing pressure takes a micro approach to making sure that others put realistic expectations on you with certain projects. But I really admire how some companies take a macro-level approach to applying appropriate expectations to their staff.

Deloitte, an international consulting firm, developed what it calls the *Mass Career Customization* (MCC) corporate career lattice. With this model, employees and managers talk through realistic expectations within the minimum to maximum range for these four areas:

- Pace of advancement (decelerated to accelerated)
- Workload (reduced to full)
- Location, travel, and schedule (restricted to not restricted)
- Role (individual contributor to leader)

Depending on the particular life circumstances of an individual, he or she can "dial up" or "dial down" in these components so he or she has the flexibility needed to balance work and life. Despite some managers' initial fears regarding everyone "dialing down" at once, the program proved successful after much testing and careful implementation. According to a *Continental Magazine*[3] article based on an interview with Cathy Benko, vice chairman at Deloitte:

> Just a year after phasing in its career lattice model, Deloitte saw among the 7,500 participants a 25 percent improvement in reported satisfaction with their career-life fit and a 28 percent increase in the number who expressed confidence about their future career-life fit. What's more, divisions that had

implemented the lattice saw their rate of employee turnover decline dramatically for high-performance personnel compared with divisions that had not implemented it.

To find out more about Deloitte's approach to realistic expectations of employees, go to www.masscareer-customization.com or check out the book on the subject: *Mass Career Customization: Aligning the Workplace with Today's Nontraditional Workforce*, by Cathy Benko and Anne C. Weisberg.

Guilt: When You Train Others to Have
Unrealistic Expectations of You

When you live a life driven by guilt, as discussed in Chapter 2, your patterns of behavior train other people to have unrealistic expectations of what you will and will not do for them and how quickly. If you typically respond to e-mails immediately, coworkers will send another e-mail when they don't hear back within a few hours. If you always take on rush orders and don't charge extra, customers will send in last-minute requests. If you pick up the phone for friends during work hours, when you're out at an event, or even when the ringing interrupts your sleep, they'll expect that they can talk to you at any time. In all these situations, you've taught people to expect certain behaviors and therefore treat you in a certain way. The good news, though, lies in the fact that you can adjust people's expectations by beginning to act differently, such as responding to e-mails in 24 hours, charging extra for rush orders, or allowing calls from friends to go to voicemail.

You also can help people to have realistic expectations of you by staying out of what I like to call *time debt*. Time debt arises when you have committed more time than you have available in one of two ways: You can accumulate literal time debt by agreeing to requests on your time before checking whether you actually have time to fulfill those requests. You also can rack up emotional time debt where you constantly tell yourself that you "should" do this or that but don't realistically have the time to do so.

When the time bills come due, such as a special customer presentation or the coordination of a school fundraiser, you panic because you've overdrawn on your time account. By saying "Yes" to too much, you encourage others to have unrealistic expectations of you.

The way to get out of time debt is to say "No" to lower priorities so that you can invest in the very best ones. Here are some examples of how my time coaching clients reset expectations:

Manager fights meeting mania. As the manager of a 50-person team with six direct reports, this corporate executive suffered from meeting overload. He had set the expectation that anyone could book a meeting on his shared calendar, and he would go to it. My client regained time during the day to answer e-mails and manage projects by starting to respond differently to meeting requests. He only accepted the absolutely most important meetings to attend, and with the rest, he took one of these approaches: asking for a copy of the meeting minutes, sending someone else in his place, or communicating his confidence in the other meeting attendees to make a decision and move forward without his presence. Not only did this help to reduce his work on nights and weekends, but it also empowered his team members.

Professor prunes piles of paper. A professor position in a scientific field at a prestigious university leads to a number of requests for your time. Some of those requests, such as teaching classes and moving ahead the lab's research, fall into the "must do" category. However, some other requests, such as certain committee work and reviewing grants and papers, aren't always mandatory. My client reduced the stress in her life by saying "No" to taking on too many paper reviews at a time. She learned that if she had already allocated the appropriate amount of time to this category of activity, it was better to graciously and quickly decline additional requests instead of saying "Yes" and ending up having her health or her own research suffer. Sending a polite, quick response gave the requesting party more time to find another reviewer and reduced guilt caused by agonizing over the decision for days.

Lawyer limits pro-bono activities. One of my clients, who also happens to have the name Elizabeth, found that her passion for children's rights and her desire to make other people happy lead to her spending more time doing pro-bono work for others than she spent investing time in building her own business. Once she realized how she put everyone else's priorities in front of her own, she delivered what she had already promised but then reset the expectations. She communicated to those asking for her time that she wouldn't complete additional pro-bono work until she had accomplished some key activities for herself.

TABLE 5.7 *Key Mental Shift: Guilt*

HARMFUL	HELPFUL
If someone asks me to do something, I must say "Yes" and take action immediately.	I have a right to say "No" to activities and to set a schedule that allows me to work at a sustainable pace.

Strengthening Your "No" Reflex

You can start resetting expectations by practicing self-restraint in terms of how quickly you respond to messages or when you answer the phone. But if it does come time—and it will—when you actually need to say "No," keep these strategies in mind:

- **Avoid offering an immediate response.** Most people's automatic reply to any request is, "Sure, I can do that." To avoid this knee-jerk reaction, always ask for time to think about your response when someone asks you about making a significant time commitment in person, over the phone, or by e-mail. Practice saying, "I really appreciate this offer but want to have the opportunity to review my other commitments before I make a decision. Would it be reasonable for me to get back to you by tomorrow afternoon?" Then be sure to follow up at that time.

- **Have a clear picture of your current responsibilities.** If you don't have a clear, comprehensive view of your schedule, you're likely to think, "I can just fit it in." But if you already know that you're booked solid,

it's easier to say "No." Keep your calendar and to-do list up-to-date so that you know how much time you really have to spend. Also, you can use a method such as the one shown in Figure 5.1 to objectively evaluate all your professional commitments. This kind of chart allows you to see what will actually fit in your schedule and where you need to cut or limit your activities.

- **Answer in a way that affirms that you value, respect, and appreciate the person.** Always thank people and, if possible, refer them to someone else who can help them. For small decisions, you can answer by e-mail. But if you're saying "No" to something large or someone important to you, try to do it by phone or in person. This gives people the opportunity to hear your "heart" behind the decision and lowers the chance of them misinterpreting your motives. If it seems appropriate, use these types of phrases:
  - "When I initially agreed to A, I didn't know about B. I really appreciate the opportunity to be involved in A. But at this time, I think it's better for you to find someone who can commit more time to this role than I can right now."
  - "Thank you for the offer, but I can't devote enough time to this initiative at present, so I think it's best for you to find someone who can better meet your needs."
  - "I already made commitments to other _____ [coworkers, clients, etc.] that I need to honor first. I will be sure to fit this in as soon as possible. Thanks for your understanding."
  - "That's not my area of expertise, but I would be happy to connect you with someone who could best help you to solve this problem."
  - "Could you e-mail me the details of that request? Once I receive them, I'll be able to give you a more definitive response on when I can get that done for you."
  - "I would love to help you out, but given my schedule, I wouldn't be able to get this back to you for a couple of weeks. If you would like to have this turned around sooner, I recommend that you reach out to _____. Does that sound good?"
- **Figure out why you fear saying "No."** Are you worried about offending people? Do you need others' approval and affirmation? Are you concerned about shutting doors? Next time you have to say "No,"

Priority	Name	Type	Hours/month	Professional Importance	Personal Satisfaction	Optional	Term (years)
	Grad student mentoring	Constant	10.00	High	High	No	Permanent
	Research	Constant	36.00	High	Medium	No	Permanent
	Teaching	Constant	48.00	Medium	Medium	No	Permanent
	Academic advising	Varied	3.33	Medium	Low	No	Permanent
	Department seminar	Constant	2.00	Medium	Low	No	Permanent
	Faculty meetings	Varied	2.00	Medium	Low	No	Permanent
	Grad admissions/recruiting	Varied	3.54	Medium	High	Yes	2
	Thesis committees	Varied	1.67	Low	Medium	Yes	3
	General PR	Varied	2.00	Low	Low	Yes	As required

Total:

Maintenance items:
  E-mails:
  Mail/phone:

Hours available: **Committed:**

FIGURE 5.1 *Example of evaluating realistic expectations for professional commitments.*

write down all the thoughts that flood into your head. Then go to Chapter 2 to find the proper tools for breaking free of these crippling emotions.

- **Discover your bigger "YES."** Make a list of the activities that are most important to you but haven't fit into your schedule because you said "Yes" too often. Every time you are tempted to overcommit, think about walking your dog, playing with your child, or simply sleeping—then say "No!"

- **Be authentic, not transparent.** I love the way Leslie Williams, author of *Leading with Grit and Grace: Smart Power for Women Leaders*, redefined authenticity as "speech and actions that arise from our deepest values" in her post for the Glass Hammer.[4] If we look at it in that form, we don't need to feel compelled to tell people why we're saying "No" to something. It's completely reasonable for you to simply say that "you're not available" because in your mind you know that if you say "Yes," you'll end up not having enough time to complete your project work, spend time with your friends, or sleep. Not having a meeting booked with someone doesn't mean that you have free time.

STRUGGLE WITH PROBLEM CUSTOMERS?

Check out my blog post on how to set expectations with clients to avoid stress: www.reallifee.com/business-owners-time-managementstress-less-by-setting-expectations-with-customers.

Your Expectations of Others:
Let Go of Resentment and Criticism

If you consistently struggle with unrealistic expectations of yourself and allow others to have unrealistic expectations of you, there's a very high probability that carries over into your having unrealistic expectations of others. These unmet expectations can cause you enormous amounts of unnecessary inner angst and outer drama, particularly with those closest to you. As you read the following two sections on resentment and criticism, do some self-examination on whether you struggle in these areas

HIGH-PAYING JOBS THAT LEAVE YOU TIME BROKE

Common wisdom: The higher your salary, the better your chances of living the life of your dreams.

Truth: There are a number of other factors that will have a profound influence on how "rich" you feel in a particular position. Consider these variables in calculating the true payoff of an opportunity and negotiating your contract:

- Tangible factors to consider:
  - How many hours you work and when
  - How much business travel is required
  - The length and cost of your commute
  - Amount of paid time off (and whether the company culture allows you to take it)
  - The cost of living in the area
  - Amount of training, mentorship, and professional development

- Less tangible factors to consider:
  - Opportunities to work from home/have a flex schedule
  - Level of variability. Is there frequent potential for unexpected demands that will keep you working late or keep you from expected time off?
  - How much mental and physical energy will the position require?
  - Will you need to spend your time off recovering from work?
  - How does this position match your need for time alone or with people?
  - Will this position drain you or fill you with energy?
  - Does your personality type and work style mesh or clash with your boss, coworkers, and the general company culture?

Conclusion: Your overall prosperity only partly correlates with your pay scale. When comparing ways of earning income, find the opportunity that will give you enough money to meet your financial goals and enough time and energy to enjoy life.

with family members, coworkers, significant others, or friends. Often we're most judgmental of those closest to us.

Resentment: When Other People Enjoy What You Want

Resentment can come in many different forms. For our purposes, though, we'll look at it in regard to when you feel upset about someone investing their time in a way that you want to—but feel you can't. This is the other side of the coin of the crippling emotion of frustration, covered in Chapter 2, where you blame others for bad things that happen to you.

With resentment, you want others to join in your suffering—"Why am I the only one at the office until 10 p.m.?"—or to help you out more—"Doesn't anyone else know how to wash dishes?"—or at least to not enjoy life so much—"How can you go to the art fair when there are weeds to pull?"

When you notice yourself getting upset when others enjoy anything good, it's time to step back for a moment and reflect on what's really happening. There may be legitimate ways you can reach out for help, such as asking for assistance with mowing the lawn or delegating more projects at work. But the root of this emotion has less to do with what others do or don't do and more to do with the fact that you need to put self-compassion in action and do a better job of taking care of yourself. If you aren't taking care of yourself—at least a little bit—99 percent of the time it's because you choose to put your needs last. Here's how Cheryl Butler, mom of eight kids and a prolific writer, put it in her Mighty Mommy post, "5 Ways That 'Selfish' Parenting Can Benefit Your Family"[5]:

> By having some sacred space that is just yours, you will teach your kids how to respect your personal boundaries. . . . I have a . . . precious nook that I can retreat to when I'm having a bad day, need some inspiration, or just want to chill, and my family has been well-trained to not disturb me when I'm in there unless the house is on fire!

If a mom of eight kids can decide it's not just okay—but essential—to take care of herself, you can too.

TABLE 5.8 *Key Mental Shift: Resentment*

HARMFUL	HELPFUL
If I don't have time to enjoy myself, others shouldn't take time to enjoy themselves either.	If I'm starting to feel resentful, I can give myself a break and take time for what I really want or need to do.

Practice Personal TLC

One of the best analogies I ever read on the importance of taking care of ourselves instead of getting upset at others comes from a book called, *The Exceptional Seven Percent: The Nine Secrets of the World's Happiest Couples*[6]:

> *Imagine that we are together, and I'm so hungry that I can't possibly wait another minute to eat. You, on the other hand, couldn't be less hungry. That leaves me two choices: I can sit around huffing and puffing, and wait for you to get hungry and make us both a meal, or I could fix myself something to eat. Of the two possibilities, the only healthy choice I can make is to accept responsibility for my need and meet it, regardless of what other alternative I might prefer.*

Let's stop blaming other people for not having an appetite and go make ourselves a sandwich, shall we?

- **Basic self-care.** Give yourself time to sleep, to eat, to exercise, to sit outside, or to do anything else that plays an essential role in your health and well-being.
- **Practice boundaries.** Stop working at a specific time, say "No," leave an event early, ask for help around the house, or simply do something less than perfectly. (It's okay to offer to bring a bottle of wine to a dinner party instead of fretting about finding mascarpone for homemade tiramisu.)
- **Spoil yourself.** Get a massage, buy the parts for the new computer you want to build, plan a weekend out-of-town trip, or do whatever else you've been longing to do but felt that you shouldn't because more important things needed to be done.

Criticism: When Others Don't Meet Your Standards

If you tend toward finding fault in others, you probably also struggle in one or both of these areas: being extremely critical of yourself or falling into the habit of judging others the way that you have been judged. Neither of these habits leads to very good results for you or for very good relationships with those around you.

In the iconic book, *How to Win Friends and Influence People,*[7] Dale Carnegie tells the story of how Abraham Lincoln matured from being an extremely critical person to adopting an attitude of humility, even when criticism may have seemed completely justified:

> *Time after time, during the Civil War, Lincoln put a new general at the head of the Army of the Potomac, and each one in turn— McClellan, Pope, Burnside, Hooker, Meade—blundered tragically and drove Lincoln to pacing the floor in despair. Half the nation savagely condemned these incompetent generals, but Lincoln, "with malice toward none, with charity for all," held his peace. One of his favorite quotations was "Judge not, that ye be not judged."*

Carnegie then goes on to tell the story of how General Meade did the opposite of what Lincoln told him to do at the Battle of Gettysburg. Meade's disobedience led to General Lee escaping when the Union Army could have triumphed victoriously. In his anger and disappointment, Lincoln wrote Meade a letter . . . but never sent it. Carnegie surmised that his restraint came from the fact that Lincoln had learned "by bitter experience that sharp criticisms and rebukes almost invariably end in futility."

TABLE 5.9 *Key Mental Shift: Criticism*

HARMFUL	HELPFUL
Why can't others measure up?	Am I using the right measuring stick?

The 3E Technique

Just as we discussed retraining your mind so that you can affirm and show compassion toward yourself, you can choose to discipline your thought

patterns to respond more kindly toward others. If you grew up in a family where you received constant criticism, intentionally reforming your thought patterns will take an immense amount of effort. But it will be worth it. You can't control what happened to you in the past, but you can decide to stop the vicious cycle and make the future different.

Also, it's important to note that you can't prevent all critical thoughts from entering your mind. But what you can do is choose whether you accept them as truth or question your critical thoughts toward someone else. The following *3E technique* can help you to process critical thoughts and help you to determine whether you have realistic expectations of others:

- **Empathize.** In this first step, you try to see the situation from the other person's point of view. You could ask yourself and, if appropriate, ask the person directly:
  - What challenges does the person face?
  - What weaknesses does the person have?
  - What people or things might have stood in the person's way?
  - What might I not know that could make a difference in how I perceive the situation?
- **Evaluate.** In this second step, you evaluate your standards and see if they are appropriate and realistic. You could think through questions such as:
  - Is what the person did truly a matter of right or wrong, good or bad, or is it simply a matter of preference?
  - If I had been facing similar pressures and circumstances, could I have responded in a similar fashion?
  - Am I actually in a close enough relationship with the person that I have the authority to evaluate his or her actions?
  - Are my standards based on perfectionist tendencies?
- **Encourage.** If you do find yourself in a position where feedback is appropriate, such as being a boss or parent, you should think through what approach would encourage the correct behavior and build the relationship:
  - How can I maintain a positive attitude toward the person and help him or her learn from mistakes and disappointments?

- What should I refrain from saying?
- What sort of feedback will the person find most motivating? Does he or she respond best to praise for positive behavior or penalties for negative behavior?
- Could I assist the person in overcoming some of the barriers he or she faces either by offering personal help or by enlisting other support?

Practice the 3E technique on a regular basis, and you'll soon find that you can respond in a calmer, more compassionate manner to those around you. If you would like to do more in-depth learning in this area, check out *How to Win Friends and Influence People* or *Crucial Confrontations.*

. . . .
Journaling Exercise: How to Escape Time Poverty and Get Time Rich *Quick*!

The Challenge
People mortgage their lives by taking on jobs or businesses with no clear boundaries on their hours, acquiring items that require extensive upkeep and maintenance, and constantly agreeing to do things they have not set aside enough time to do.

The Solution
Thinking about and tracking your time as a tangible asset that you purposefully allocate to high-value activities.

TABLE 5.10 *Key Mental Shift: Time Wealthy*

Harmful	Helpful
I should be able to make time for everything.	Time is a limited resource.
I will always be time poor.	I can choose to get out of time debt.
I'll just "fit in" important activities when I have time.	If I don't plan important activities, they probably won't happen.

Journaling Question

When will you begin to take action in each of these areas?

- Make a brutally honest assessment of how much time you have and how much you've committed to spend.

- Ruthlessly cut nonessential activities.

- Start saying "No" to all but the very best opportunities.

- When you add something to your schedule, take something out.

- Plan in basic life-sustaining activities, such as sleep, first.

- Develop a clear planning routine that allows you to slow down and strategically reallocate your time resources on a regular basis.

- Realize that you won't make everyone happy—but you will make yourself and the most important people in your life happiest when you invest your time well.

. . . .

Notes

1. Alan Chapman, "Personality Theories, Types and Tests," Businessballs.com. Available at: www.businessballs.com/personalitystylesmodels.htm#benziger%20 brain-types%20and%20personality%20theory.

2. Tara Parker-Pope, "Go Easy on Yourself, a New Wave of Research Urges," *New York Times*. Available at: http://well.blogs.nytimes.com/2011/02/28/go -easy-on-yourself-a-new-wave-of-research-urges.

3. Erik Sherman, "Climbing the Corporate Lattice," *Continental Magazine*, November 2010, pp. 54–56.

4. Leslie Williams, "It's Time to Redefine Authenticity," Evolved People Media. Available at: www.theglasshammer.com/news/2011/01/26/its-time-to -redefine-authenticity.

5. Cheryl Butler, "5 Ways That 'Selfish Parenting' Can Benefit Your Family," Quick and Dirty Tips. Available at: http://mightymommy.quickanddirtytips.com/selfish-parenting-improves-family-life.aspx.

6. Gregory K. Popcak, *The Exceptional Seven Percent: The Nine Secrets of the World's Happiest Couples*. New York: Kensington Publishing, 2000.

7. Dale Carnegie, *How to Win Friends and Influence People*. New York: Simon & Schuster, 2009.

CHAPTER 6

SECRET #3

Strengthen Simple Routines

Habit is either the best of servants or the worst of masters.

—NATHANIEL EMMONS, AMERICAN THEOLOGIAN

Routines Create a Natural Flow: My Morning Routine

My internal clock is set to 6 a.m. This is awesome on weekdays because it's usually not a problem for me to get up when my alarm goes off. It's not so awesome on the weekends when I've stayed up later than 11 p.m. and want to sleep in—but can't.

If I wake up with unpleasant thoughts in my head (perhaps from a weird dream), I sometimes lie in bed a bit past 6 a.m. so that I can process the negative emotions. I then get up and immediately grab my Bible and my journal from my nightstand and take them downstairs to the dining room and put them in my designated spot.

I love that the house is quiet and I'm alone at this hour. It's very peaceful, and my mind can wander and get lost in thoughts without interruption. I start my fabulous Bunn coffee maker (only four minutes to brew a whole pot!) and then put together a simple breakfast and take out my vitamins.

As I gather my food, I make a rough sketch in my mind of what I plan on eating for breakfast, lunch, and dinner. That way, I know that I'm getting some variety in my three meals and enough nutrients from fruits and vegetables. I also make note of anything that I need to buy on my "Grocery List" note on my phone.

Now it's time to sit down and eat. As I munch, I read a short passage from my Bible and then take time to ponder what it means to me. Usually, during my pondering time, I go back for seconds on breakfast food. (I eat my food on small serving dishes so that I can go back for more without guilt!)

Next, I take time to meditate for about an hour. Depending on my mood, this can take many different forms:

- Writing in a prayer journal
- Listening to an affirmations CD
- Lying on the living room floor, staring at the ceiling, and sorting out my thoughts
- Going on a walk through my neighborhood

After my meditation time, I'm typically feeling peaceful, energized, and prepared to face the day. Around 7:30 a.m., I start to transition from *being* to *doing*. I put away the breakfast food and clean up any dishes. I go around the house fluffing pillows, shutting cabinets, gathering up stray items, and generally reassuring myself that everything is in order in my physical environment so that I can more or less ignore it for the next eight hours.

If I need to leave the house for an appointment during work hours, I shower and get ready for the day completely. (I have a tendency to underestimate how long it can take to get ready and get out of the house.) If I'm not going out until the evening, I just put on clothes for going on a walk at lunch and leave doing my hair, makeup, and jewelry until the end of the day so that everything is "fresh."

Sometime between 8 and 8:30 a.m., I sit down at my computer and begin my morning processing and planning routine.

My wake-up ritual is specifically designed to make getting out of bed, spending time in prayer and meditation, eating well, and feeling good about my physical environment as easy as possible. I don't need to think about what will happen and when. I simply go through the motions. Your morning routine may look very different from mine, but ideally it creates the same sort of natural flow as you start your day.

Routines don't need to be highly scripted regimens that make you feel like a soldier at boot camp or a grade school child under the tyranny of a

shrill bell. But they do need to be intentionally developed and strengthened so that effective time investment comes as easily as possible.

Secret #3: Strengthen Simple Routines

Here's the truth: Habit patterns rule. If you haven't yet discovered the secret of strengthening simple routines for automatic time investment, the world of the organized and efficient appears to be some far-off dream world unattainable by mere mortals. From the outside looking in, it seems like those on "the other side" instinctively know what to do—and not do—at every moment. They naturally choose to invest their time well. They can instantly compute the cost of their choices, and the flow of their life effortlessly moves them toward their highest goals. This is why Secret #3 is *strengthen simple routines*. Let's break down the three parts:

Strengthen. *To make stronger, to reinforce.* In some ways, the preceding assessment rings true. Those who have strengthened simple routines that naturally lead them toward their action-based priorities and realistic expectations operate at a high level of efficiency without a great deal of conscious thought about their actions. Fortunately, anyone can choose to create and reinforce new patterns of behavior in their lives. What you'll need to do is to repeatedly choose to act and think in a new way. This repetition will then build your time-management strength in the same way that weight training enhances your muscle strength.

Simple. *Easily understood or done.* Simple routines increase your capacity to handle life because they reduce the number of decisions you need to make and give you confidence that you're making the right time investment choice for the moment. As I illustrated in the table at the beginning of Chapter 5, complex routines, such as wanting to cook an elaborate meal instead of putting together some spaghetti and sauce, can lead to overwhelm. Start with very basic routines that you can sustain over time. Then, as you build your capacity, you can elaborate on them.

Routines. *A sequence of actions regularly followed.* Routines act as standard operating procedures that make flowing through daily activities, responding to inputs, and moving forward on important

goals as close to effortless as possible. If you thrive on spontaneity, the concept of following routines may seem about as appealing as having teeth pulled. But hear me out on this: Practicing routines for the regular activities of life, such as sleep, exercise, grocery shopping, and answering e-mail, actually gives you more freedom to be flexible. How, so you ask? The key is that when you make the mundane details of life effortless, you have more time and energy to devote to other parts of your life. Instead of worrying about whether your bills are paid, you can do proactive activities like investing in a small business or planning a trip.

TABLE 6.1 *Key Mental Shift: Simple Routines*

HARMFUL	HELPFUL
If I just make more lists, I'll remember everything.	I need to create natural triggers in my life that prompt me to start a familiar routine.
If I'm just more disciplined and exert more willpower, I can do what I want to do.	I need to make my routines as effortless as possible, breaking down change into incremental steps and removing barriers.

Routines Increase a Sense of Control

Here's an example of how one of my time coaching clients learned how applying Secret #3 could help him to feel in control and stay focused: When my soon-to-be client reached out to me, he had a lot going for him, such as:

- A cool job at a small biotech company
- A lot of flexibility in his hours
- Tons of variety in his work, including some graphic design
- Dogs and cats that made him happy
- Volunteer opportunities with a local political organization

The only problem was that he couldn't enjoy any of it because he constantly felt overloaded. As he said in his initial e-mail to me:

I know I have so much potential, but I try to make everyone happy, and I lose out. I think the better I get at things, the less time I have. Now I'm getting too good, and I'm suffering for it. It feels like some kind of ceiling. . . . I never have time for anything. What would you recommend for me?

After completing an initial phone consultation, my client and I agreed that working together to develop better routines was the right solution. Each week, we talked through a specific challenge and developed a new routine for him to implement. We focused on key activities that would reduce his stress level and increase his sense of satisfaction with life, such as daily planning, exercising, getting to bed earlier, and having time for friends on the weekends. Here's what he discovered:

I can't believe how small, incremental changes really made a difference in my thought process about being organized. I learned not to be so hard on myself and that I don't have to be so strict about organizing. There is a gray area where I do have a choice on whether I adhere to fixed schedules or not. That made the process a whole lot less stressful.

I also realized how irrational the procrastinating "voices" are and how being more organized and more focused can make not only my life less stressful but also the lives of those around me.

After my client established his initial routines, we continued to make refinements to further increase his sense of control and balance. For instance, during one session, we discussed how he was doing better at setting reasonable turn-around deadlines when he received requests through e-mail. But when someone asked him for something in person, his knee-jerk response was still to always agree to a short deadline.

To address this challenge, we talked through his mind-set and developed a better automatic response. Here's the script we developed that still made him seem approachable and respectful but gave him time to think through his answer about projects: "If you send me the details in

an e-mail, it will be easier for me to give you a definitive answer. Does that sound reasonable?"

I'm really proud of my client for the changes he's made in his life. Not only is he more effective at work, but he's also focused on not burning himself out so that he can actually have a life outside the office. We've wrapped up our coaching together, but he continues to have the support of his new time investment routines. Here's what he had to say about his experience:

> *Work has been less stressful, and I've been more productive and efficient. I worry less about missing something important. I get more exercise by walking the dogs more often, and I'm working on things that I had put off for months or even years. . . . Having gone from disorganized and stressed to sane and more relaxed, I honestly don't know what could have made the experience any better.*

This client's natural tendency was to fall into a reactive method of time management, where he felt pushed around by external circumstances. But did you see how simple routines had such a positive impact on his life?

He could dramatically decrease his stress level and improve the experience of those around him because he was willing to regularly practice small, incremental changes. This graphic designer didn't need to put his life in a straight jacket or stop being helpful to other people. He simply needed to strengthen simple routines that allowed him to have an internal sense of control about what happened with his schedule. This allowed him to respond with agility to a variety of complex requests at a small biotech business and not feel like his flexible schedule was a work-all-the-time schedule.

I love the way Tom Robbins puts it in this quote: "True stability results when presumed order and presumed disorder are balanced. A truly stable system expects the unexpected, is prepared to be disrupted, and waits to be transformed."

TABLE 6.2 *Key Mental Shift: Internal Control*

HARMFUL	HELPFUL
I have so many requests on my time from so many different people, which makes any sort of routine impossible.	When I follow a routine, I'm better able to handle the many requests on my time and also to set the appropriate boundaries and expectations.

FACEBOOK COO LEAVES WORK AT 5:30 P.M.[1]

When you have an incredible amount of responsibility at work like Sheryl Sandberg, the COO of Facebook, routines that support your action-based priorities become even more essential. To reflect her priority of family, she chooses the action of coming home for family dinner and establishes the routine of leaving the office at 5:30 p.m. to arrive home by 6 p.m. If Sheryl hadn't strengthened that routine, it would be easy to fall into the trap of many executives who say family is a priority but rarely see their spouse or children.

Routines Build Momentum on Big, Scary Projects

Although routines can slow down the pace of life and decrease the number of hours that overwhelmed individuals need to work, they also can create momentum for those who aren't working enough. Some of the individuals who struggle with this issue the most are creative professionals, students, salespeople, and entrepreneurs who work from home on challenging, unclear projects where the results they will achieve are uncertain.

They feel horribly embarrassed about their lack of productivity because they know that they have time to move forward but don't know when and how to start. Also, they usually have some fear associated with doing the work or having their results judged. Fortunately, strengthening simple routines can help them to break months—or even years—of delay.

Here's an example of how simple routines empowered one of my time coaching clients to make progress on a long-delayed book: Starting a new

project in an area where you have excelled but almost killed yourself in the process is terrifying. . . .

- What if you can't produce the same level of results?
- What if you lose yourself and quality relationships in the process?
- What if you end up feeling terrible the entire time you're doing the work?

These are all valid concerns when your past experience tells you that the only way to get big projects done is to work at a frenzied pace.

Fortunately, there's a better way.

Last winter, I worked with a successful, well-published writer who also taught in a university graduate school masters of fine arts program. She was stuck: "I am scattered and making erratic progress with this or that. I want to make solid steps forward. I want to reclaim my life and place in the literary firmament, get healthy and in shape, and have fun!"

This client also had just been diagnosed with attention deficit hyperactivity disorder (ADHD) and was wondering how much of an impact ADHD had on her lifelong frustrations with writing and other areas of her life. One of her most important goals was to move forward on her next big creative project—a collection of linked short stories. It had been a long time since her first book had been published, and she needed to regain professional momentum.

> *My friends are mostly writers and successful. I have lots of ink in* The New York Times *that I have written and that has been written about me. So I have talent. I also need to know what I need to do, like a solid schedule? Work impulsively? Okay, I know the answer to that.*

She did know the answer, but turning the answer into practical action took developing and strengthening simple routines. We came up with an initial plan of how she could get a good, solid block of writing time in every morning. Then, each week, we worked on assessing the results and evaluating how to move forward based on what had happened. Here is my client's reflection on the changes I helped her make in her life:

I found the process very stabilizing because I tend to be all over the place with trying things. It was helpful having you to run things off of, especially when I got stuck—which was about every week.

We worked together on different morning writing routines. The first involved drinking coffee, eating breakfast, taking the dog out, meditating, getting dressed, and then starting to write. The second involved just getting coffee and starting to write. The end result was a fusion of the two, with pouring a cup of coffee, meditating a bit, taking the dog out, and then writing.

The end goal wasn't to have this creative writer crammed into a rigid schedule but rather to have something that turned writing (her top professional priority) from a dreaded activity into a peaceful part of her daily schedule. Over the course of six months, she found that if she followed her morning routine and put herself in her writing space for two hours (with a timer set), the inspiration came, and the writing moved forward.

- Writing didn't need to be something that she dreaded.
- Writing didn't need to be something that took over her life.
- Writing could be something she chose to move forward with each day.

At last! Freedom to do quality work without losing herself, her relationships, or her sanity!

I've found that the actual schedule that I longed for would absolutely drive me around the bend, so I have a flexitarian schedule and am getting things done. Having and sticking with a schedule is the single most important thing I can do for myself as an artist, as a woman living a rather complex and exciting life, and as someone newly aware that many of my problems stem from having ADHD. Nothing, nothing, nothing will move me forward like following my schedule will. Period.

The same could be true for you. You can take away the fear surrounding moving forward on a big project by developing, practicing, and adjusting your own simple routines. The beauty of routine, particularly for creative professionals and other sorts of knowledge workers, is that it gives them the ability to regularly move forward on their work, get lost

in the flow, and also stop without guilt or fear that they won't have the ability to start again. Knowing that life is in order and that the time set aside for a project is the right investment at the moment gives you the freedom to transcend from the mundane details of life into the sublime.

TABLE 6.3 *Key Mental Shift: Big Project Momentum*

HARMFUL	HELPFUL
The only way to make progress on a big project is to completely throw myself into it and neglect my needs and my relationships.	When I follow a routine, I can make consistent, peaceful progress on a big project without sacrificing my health or key relationships.

How to Pacify Your Inner Routine Rebel

Despite these illustrations of the value of routine, you may still feel a very strong resistance to change. That's understandable. If you prefer to go with the flow, it's natural to feel skeptical and rebellious. So, before we move forward in the next chapter with practical action steps for creating and strengthening simple routines, let's take some time to slow down and address what's really going on below the surface.

Your thoughts and feelings matter. I'm not going to ignore them, invalidate them, or diminish their importance. But I am going to encourage you that you have a choice of how you respond to the defensiveness that tends to spring up when you're asked to think differently, feel differently, or act differently. With consistent, intentional choice, you can overcome your emotional immune system's natural response to the idea of developing routines.

Here's a list of common internal struggles that can hold you back from change and how you can decide to reply to them. You can print a copy of these phrases at www.reallifee.com/tib to post in the places you most struggle with following routine. To further drive the point home, you can say these phrases out loud or simply repeat them in your head to pacify your inner routine rebel:

> **But I don't like routine.** I don't have to like routine. But I can choose to incorporate it into my life to create more of the peace, joy, and sense of control that I really want to experience.

Routines will hinder my creativity. Routines give me more time to set aside for my creative work because I'm more efficient at getting other things done. Also, I'm better able to enter the "flow state" because I'm not worrying about what I might be forgetting.

SUPERCHARGED INNOVATION

Worried that routine will squelch your ability to innovate? Think again. Companies such as 3M with its 15 percent time[2] and Google with its 20 percent time[3] plan time for employees to pursue projects outside their core job responsibilities. This means that innovation becomes part of everyone's weekly routine instead of getting pushed aside in pursuit of the current, urgent matters.

I'll miss out on opportunities. I do not need to make my entire life routine! I can just choose to add structure where I most need it to reduce stress.

I might not feel like doing what I planned to do. I always have a choice of whether I follow my routine, but routine allows me to more easily and consistently move forward on what's most important to me. Routine helps me to do what I want to do even when I don't long to do it.

I don't like knowing what's coming next. I can plan routines, schedule prompts (such as reminder e-mails, alarms, or even people), and then forget about what I planned. Then it still feels like a surprise.

Routines make me feel rebellious. The right amount of structure empowers me to stop worrying about the mundane details of life and frees me to achieve my full potential and to focus on exciting new ventures. Routine is my gravitational pull that keeps me from flying out of orbit. I can practice essential routines when I need them and reward myself with totally spontaneous time outside those parameters.

Routines make me feel like a victim. I have the ability to choose what I include in my routines. I can decide to invest only in routines that are aligned with my personal definition of success and based

on realistic expectations. My routines are my servants, not my masters.

Routines make life boring. I have choice in how I perform routine activities. For example, I can choose to exercise a different way each day, or I can spend my writing time in different locations. I can also use routine to decrease negative stress and increase opportunities for new experiences and spontaneity—such as room for a new relationship or a trip.

FREEDOM MAXIMIZATION

Jenny Blake, author of *Life After College* and lifestyle entrepreneur extraordinaire, uses routines to maximize the amount of freedom that she has in her life. For example, she schedules her coaching clients for one to two days a week so that she can focus on other business priorities on the other days. She leaves the nights and weekends free so that she can entertain friends and organize groups such as "Geek Yoga." Also, she took a self-described "Eat, Pray, Yoga" journey through Asia and put up an autoresponder that told people to resend messages to her after her return if they desired a reply. Routine gives Jenny the ability to maximize life's potential for adventure.

Sometimes I just need to rest. I can put rest into my routine on a regular basis. I also have the choice to make exceptions to the routine.

If I can't follow the routine perfectly, I don't want to try at all. Developing routines takes time and practice—kind of like learning to ride a bike or speak a language. I can still see value in making progress, and over time, my practice can lead me closer and closer to perfect.

If I plan something and then don't follow through, I'll feel like a failure. My plans and routines are not meant as a judgment but as a way for me to know how to focus, to track my progress, and to evaluate the results. When I don't achieve the desired results, I can reflect on what I can choose to do differently next time without engaging in self-criticism.

I can't focus for long periods. I tend to get distracted. I can limit the length of time that I need to devote to a particular activity and factor time for distraction into my routine. I can also have routines such as going to places without Internet access to decrease the level of temptation.

ENHANCED FOCUS

For more tips on the routines that allow you to craft your optimal work environment, check out my blog post entitled, "Setting the Scene for a Productive Day," at www.99U.com/tips/7093/Setting-the-Scene-for-a-Productive-Day.

I can only keep a routine for a couple of days or weeks. Then I fall off track. I can choose to put the right accountability, support, and encouragement into place to help keep me motivated with practicing my routines.

What if I'm not able to keep my whole routine because I'm sick, on vacation, or something else comes up? I can develop an alternate routine for times when I'm not able to complete the full routine. Also, I always have a choice to decide whether the new activity that came up is of more value to me than sticking with my original routine.

SUMMER FUN

You can choose to have a more relaxed routine on your "off-season" that allows you to recharge and prepare for your busy times. Here's how Marie Forleo, marketing and lifestyle expert, puts it: "Summer is officially in session. For me, that means much shorter workdays and a lot more time cooking, chilling at the beach, reading, and gardening. It's my core time to recharge and reconnect with what's really important. I also like to look ahead at what I want to create in the upcoming year."[4]

I can't do this, so why should I even try? Each day I can choose to take small steps in the direction of my goals. I am capable of making progress and building my capacity to the right level for my personality and needs.

People always mess with my routines. I may need to adjust and adapt my routines to accommodate the changes created by others around me. But even implementing some type of routine puts me in a better place than not implementing any routine at all. I can also choose to set boundaries and help people to understand why I need to follow these routines.

I can just sleep less. Living in a perpetually sleep-deprived state is an unsustainable, unhealthy way of life. Pushing myself to stay up late hurts my overall productivity, increases my stress, and leads to lower-quality results.

Did any of these phrases sound familiar? If so, you've got an inner routine rebel that needs to adjust his or her attitude and then get to work on strengthening the right simple routines.

Routines Require Intentional Practice

At first it will take a great deal of mental and emotional fortitude to even want to start putting these routines into practice. Then, once you do begin implementation, new routines will feel difficult because you have to consciously choose to do something different than your subconscious naturally chose to do in the past. It's like hacking a new pathway through the jungle of the day when you were used to strolling down a well-established trail or like breaking up scar tissue and retraining your muscles when your body developed bad compensation techniques after an injury.

The process hurts. It's draining at first.

Ultimately, though, strengthening simple routines leads to a life where you consistently achieve more success with less stress. I really appreciate how Cal Newport, popular productivity blogger and prolific author, most recently of *So Good They Can't Ignore You: Why Skills Trump Passion in the Quest for Work You Love*, explained the concept of deliberate practice as a key element in creating a remarkable life. In his post entitled, "The

Father of Deliberate Practice Disowns Flow,"[5] Cal included this excerpt from an article by Anders Ericsson and Paul Ward published in *Current Directions in Psychological Science*[6]:

> *It is clear that skilled individuals can sometimes experience highly enjoyable states ("flow" as described by Mihaly Csikszentmihalyi, 1990) during their performance. These states are, however, incompatible with deliberate practice, in which individuals engage in a (typically planned) training activity aimed at reaching a level just beyond the currently attainable level of performance by engaging in full concentration, analysis after feedback, and repetitions with refinement.*

Cal then provided this commentary on the research findings:

> *The feeling of flow is different than the feeling of getting better. If all you seek is flow, then you're not going to get better. There is no avoiding the deliberate strain of real improvement. (This is not to say, however, that you should not seek flow in addition to deliberate practice as a strategy to recharge, or experience it as unavoidable when you put your deliberately honed skills to use.)*

TABLE 6.4 *Key Mental Shift: Intentional Practice*

HARMFUL	HELPFUL
If something doesn't feel fun or natural from the beginning, it's wrong and unsustainable.	My new routines may feel awkward at first, but as I practice them, they will become more natural and comfortable.

Strengthening simple routines does require effort, but it's possible and worth it. Here's how one of my time coaching clients who works as an employee at a Fortune 500 company described the process of learning to keep up his time investment routines:

> *I'm getting more disciplined about time blocking (progress!). But one of the things that good time blocking does is make you aware of*

how little discretionary time you actually have to spend. So I started thinking about: "Where can I cut back on something I'm doing?" Immediately I thought of exercise. When you include travel, changing, showering, etc., most of my workout sessions are almost two hours. But then, almost instantly, I said to myself, "No, that's not negotiable. I'm not going to cut back on exercise because it brings me so many benefits in terms of my energy level, my long-term health, and even the emotional value of validating the worth of self-care." Then it hit me—I'm struggling to "find the time" to purge my index cards, time block my day, and do good weekly reviews. But this wouldn't take me hours a day. I find the time for exercise; why not time management? I thought of a few reasons:

1. *At some level, I'm still not convinced that I'll see the deep benefits. Rationally, I believe there will be benefits. But since I haven't experienced the higher state, I don't have enough evidence to have a deep emotional connection with the benefits.*

2. *I've worked at exercising for years and seen the benefits of exercising and the negative results of not exercising. I know the magnitude of the benefits of exercising because of the contrast at various times. I haven't had the same history and experience with time management.*

3. *I know how to exercise, and I've done it enough that I'm good at it. Exercise feels good, and I feel good about being good at it. I've also got lots of things down to a routine and set up to make it easy. I own enough exercise clothes that I don't have to worry about laundry. I've had my workout routines designed by a fitness center trainer, so I'm confident I'm doing things that will work. I have my checklist for packing my exercise clothes, and it's part of my daily routine. I know what times of day I can usually fit it in, and part of looking over my daily landscape is figuring out when to fit in exercise. I don't really question whether or not I want to fit it in: It's a "given."*

With time management, in many ways I'm still a novice: I don't feel like I'm really good at it and just don't have enough history and experience as to how to respond to the various challenges. Therefore:

1. *I need to focus on simple things I can do, make them very con-crete, and keep practicing until I get good. I need to be patient and gentle with myself, not set an extremely aggressive goal and then beat myself up when I don't reach it. It's the equivalent of starting to exercise by walking around the block once, then twice, then working up to where you can do 20 to 30 minutes of intense aerobics.*

2. *It takes time; you need to be patient with yourself. You have to have the belief that the benefits are there if you keep going, and holding onto that belief is one of the key challenges. Another thought I got from the book* Drive *is that "Mastery is painful." To get really, really good at something, you have to have extremely disciplined practice over an extended period of time, like the NBA player who shoots 500 foul shots at the end of every practice.*

As my client so eloquently described, lasting change in your routines is possible. Ultimately, though, it will come down to you choosing to move ahead and keep at it even when the process seems like a struggle. With practice, investing your time well will be your natural path of least resistance and lead you toward your action-based priorities and realistic expectations.

In Chapter 7, I'll walk you step-by-step through the process of how to create your own simple routines. For a jump-start, you can also flip to the "Quick Reference Done-For-You Routines and Tools" at the end of Chapter 7 for sample routines in categories such as sleep, exercise, and e-mail. Before we get into action, though, here's one final exercise to help put you in the correct mind-set for success with routines.

. . . .
Journaling Exercise: Hard to Swallow

Your associations with "organized people" may make time invest-ment advice hard to swallow. Let me explain: When I go to a new restaurant or I'm in a new place, I try to eat new foods. Some cuisine I find delicious. But other dishes I literally can't swallow because I'm so disturbed at the thought of what's in them. Objec-

tively, the food might be tasty, but I'm emotionally repulsed by the mental association.

The same power of association holds true in other areas. If you have negative associations with organized people or with the results of good time investment, such as having free time, it will be really hard for you to swallow any advice that will lead you toward something you find *so* distasteful.

Journaling Questions

To uncover whether any of these biases may be holding you back from success, ponder these points:

- When I imagine an "organized person," who comes to mind?
  - What type of feelings do I have toward this person?
  - What adjectives would I use to describe him or her?
  - What do I like and dislike about this individual?
  - Do I want to be like this person? If so, why? If not, why not?

- When I imagine myself being organized, what images come to mind?
  - Are there any feelings other than peace and joy?
  - Is there any sense of guilt or fear?
  - Is there any worry that I'll lose my value if I'm not serving or sacrificing or stressed enough?
  - Is there any resistance to letting go of daily drama?

If these questions uncover strong emotional and mental associations that may lead you to self-sabotage your attempts to change, try this exercise for welcoming a positive image of an organized person:

- Think about what kind of person you dread becoming by investing your time effectively.

- Imagine a beautiful, peaceful, organized setting.

- Envision the kind of organized person you would like to be who has many positive qualities such as being peaceful, kind, helpful, patient, and so on.

- Now go and put the unpleasant organized person into the beautiful, peaceful setting.

- Once that's done, watch as the positive organized person walks into the beautiful setting and says, "Please leave. I'm the new vision of organization."

- Then observe as the negative organized person departs.

- Finally, allow yourself to spend a few moments with the positive organized person in the beautiful, peaceful setting.

This visualization process helps you to form new patterns of association, gives you a positive vision of who you could be, and propels you toward that ideal future. You also can seek out role models who embody both effective time investment and the other qualities you want to possess. If you ever start to feel anxious about who you would become if you were organized, go through this journaling exercise again. Following routines doesn't have to mean losing yourself!

. . . .

Notes

1. Jessica Stillman, "Sheryl Sandberg Leaves Work at 5:30. Why Can't You?" *Inc.* Available at: www.inc.com/jessica-stillman/facebook-sheryl-sandberg-can-leave-early-why-arent-you.html.

2. Kaomi Goetz, "How 3M Gave Everyone Days Off and Created an Innovation Dynamo," Co.Design. Available at: www.fastcodesign.com/1663137/how-3m-gave-everyone-days-off-and-created-an-innovation-dynamo.

3. Alexia Tsotsis, "Google's '20 Percent Time' Will Survive the Death of Google Labs," AOLTech. Available at: http://techcrunch.com/2011/07/20/20-percent.

4. Marie Forleo, "3 Secrets for Building Wealth: Interview with Amanda Steinberg from DailyWorth.com," Marie Forleo International. Available at: http://marieforleo.com/2012/06/wealth-building-secrets/#ixzz1yYcjGelM.

5. Cal Newport, "The Father of Deliberate Practice Disowns Flow," Study Hacks. Available at: http://calnewport.com/blog/2012/04/09/the-father-of-deliberate-practice-disowns-flow.

6. Anders Ericsson and Paul Ward, "Capturing the Naturally Occurring Superior Performance of Experts in the Laboratory," *Current Directions in Psychological Science* 16(6), 2007: 346-350.

THE IMPLEMENTATION

CHAPTER 7

HOW TO CREATE
YOUR OWN ROUTINES

A Step-by-Step Guide

*Unless you try to do something beyond what you have
already mastered, you will never grow.*

—RALPH WALDO EMERSON, AMERICAN ESSAYIST,
LECTURER, AND POET

Four Essential Steps

By this point, you should be fairly confident that strengthening simple
routines will create massive benefits in your life. (If you're not convinced
yet, you probably skipped Chapter 6. Back up, read it, and then come
back to this spot. Are you ready now? Good.) The time for intellectual
agreement with theories has passed, and it's time to get serious about
implementation.

So . . . routines. At their simplest, they look like the way you pour coffee into your favorite mug each morning or the parking spot you drive to
first. At their most complex, they look like your method for approaching
annual tax filings. Simply put, routines are the habitual way you perform
recurring activities.

If you shower, eat, and sleep somewhat regularly, you've already got
a whole repertoire of routines for daily living. If you're engaged in some
type of productive activity at work, school, or home, that's also a sign that
you have even more routines in place that allow you not only to function
but also to contribute to the world.

In some areas, though, you may not have achieved the results you desire, or the routines that once worked for you may no longer take you to where you want to go. This could come as a result of a change in you—such as getting older, taking on more responsibilities, or being sick—or a change around you—such as having a child, buying a house, or economic upheaval. To achieve more success with less stress in these circumstances, you need to intentionally craft and then strengthen simple routines that create new paths of least resistance in your life. In the following pages you'll discover how you can create your own routines in these four steps:

- **Step 1**: Prepare for action.
- **Step 2**: Anticipate everything.
- **Step 3**: Practice the routine.
- **Step 4**: Review, reward, and recalibrate.

Following these step-by-step instructions, I've included "Create Your Own Routine" and "Simple Project Plan" templates, and you can download digital versions of them at www.reallifee.com/tib. I tried to make this guide as comprehensive as possible, but feel free to create routines with as much or as little detail as you need to achieve your priorities. This chapter also contains a library of done-for-you routines that show you real-life examples from my clients and other special contributors. Now let's get started!

Step 1: Prepare for Action

Identify Your Priority Areas

Not all routines need to be optimized. Yes, some people turn sorting their socks into a 20-step procedure, but that may or may not be the most effective investment of your time. When you're looking at adding or changing routines in your life, begin by deciding what's most important to you now. You can review what you discovered about your action-based priorities in Chapter 4 and then make a decision about which area to focus on first based on these types of questions:

- What do I have the ability to start on right now?

- What really bothers me on a regular basis?
- What would make me feel really proud of myself if I accomplished it?

Example: I would really like to make my health a priority because it bothers me that I am always tired. I would be really proud of myself for practicing more healthy habits.

My priority area is:

. . . .

Build Change or Embrace Change

In order to successfully integrate in new routines, you need to use a strategy that suits your personality type and natural inclinations. Here are two different approaches that I have seen work. Pick the one that best reflects your actual tendencies, not just what you think you "should" do.

- **Building change strategy.** You do best by *building change* if you prefer to do one new activity and get to a certain degree of comfort with it before moving on to the next activity. When integrating new routines, you should focus on just one new routine at a time and then gradually add in others. Typically, one new routine a week is manageable, but you can go faster or slower depending on how comfortable you feel in the moment.
  Example: I will focus on exercising regularly. Once I am working out consistently, then I will focus on eating fruits and vegetables daily.
- **Embracing change strategy.** You do best by *embracing change* if you feel motivated by taking on a whole cluster of new routines all at once. When someone tells you that you can only work on one activity at a time, you feel stifled and disinterested. When you can throw yourself into a large set of activities, though, you can't wait to get started.
  Example: I will exercise regularly, drink eight glasses of water each day, cut out sweets from my diet, and get to bed by 11 p.m.

I prefer this approach to change:

. . . .

Special note: If you prefer to embrace change, go through the following steps for each one of the routines in your cluster of activities. Then enjoy implementing them all at once. If you prefer building change, wait to come up with your next custom routine until you've started to feel successful with your first one.

Clarify the Actions

As discussed in Chapter 4, the path to authentically living out your priorities is to display total commitment to the specific actions that will make your priorities a priority in your time investment. It's insufficient data for your brain to simply say, "I will exercise regularly." What your brain needs to know is what action your body needs to take to make this happen and the exact definition of success.

Examples of what this could sound like in the case of "I will exercise regularly" include:

- On Monday, Wednesday, and Friday, I will leave work by 6 p.m. and go to the gym, where I will do 30 minutes of aerobic activity and 20 minutes of strength training.
- Three days a week, I will spend one hour doing some sort of sporty activity, which could include running, playing basketball, or kayaking.
- Each morning before I leave for work, I will walk outside for 20 minutes.

Special note: For some very important priorities, such as your relationships, the exact actions can seem less obvious. Here are the types of activities that you could do to make relationships a priority:

- I will stop working by 6:30 p.m. every evening so that I can have dinner with my significant other.
- Each week, I will have at least one intentional, uninterrupted one-on-one conversation with each person in my family.
- On a monthly basis, I will reach out to my close friends and schedule a time to talk with them or meet with them.

I will take this action:

. . . .

Ready Your Equipment and Supplies

Now it's time to decide exactly what equipment and supplies you will need to complete the desired action.

Example: Walking shoes, workout clothes, water bottle

I need this equipment and these supplies:

. . . .

Then put the equipment and supplies into these categories:

Ready to go: . . . .

To buy: . . . .

To borrow: . . . .

To find: . . . .

To clean: . . . .

To prepare: . . . .

Special note: To *prepare* supplies or equipment refers to items such as exercise equipment that you need to assemble. For any of the items that aren't in the *ready to go* category, you need to clarify what next steps need to happen and then decide on a specific day and time when you will move forward on these steps. To help you with this, I have included a "Simple Project Plan" template at the end of the chapter that you can also download from www.reallifee.com/tib.

Create Your Ideal Environment

Knowing that you have a place to practice your routine where you can expect a consistent experience lowers your resistance to forming a new habit. Typically, therefore, it works best to pick one ideal environment. But if you're someone who likes more spontaneity and variety, then you can develop a set of places where you can strengthen your new routine.

Example: I will walk around my neighborhood on the streets with sidewalks.

If you already have an optimal space to do what you need to get done, fabulous. Write it here and move on to the next section.

My ideal environment is:

. . . .

If you don't have a good place in mind and/or the environment you have is less than ideal (i.e., instead of encouraging you to follow your routine, it works against you in various ways), then make note of what you would need to do in each one of these categories to create your ideal environment:

What I need to find:

. . . .

What I need to create or build:

. . . .

What I need to change:

. . . .

What I need to clean:

. . . .

What I need to eliminate:

. . . .

What I need to communicate to the other people who share the space:

. . . .

The last point relates to letting other people know if and when they should be in the space and how you expect them to treat it. For instance, let's say that you assembled your treadmill, cleared the area around it, and placed it in a position where you could see the TV so that you could easily exercise every day before work. But then the people who live with you decide that the treadmill would make a convenient drying rack for their laundry. Despite your valiant efforts, your attempts to create your ideal environment would be thwarted. In order to preserve the place you created, you need to set boundaries with them. That way you can have confidence that the treadmill will be ready when it's time for you to do your exercise routine.

Now, once again, I would like you to clarify the actions required for anything that fell into the *need to* categories and assign a day and time when you will move forward on these steps. If you find it helpful, you can use the "Simple Project Plan" template for each one.

Find Information and Learn Skills

Uncertainty about exactly how to do something can cause you to avoid strengthening a new routine. Although you should watch out for perpetual delays caused by always wanting to "do more research," sometimes you do have a legitimate need to find out more information or learn new skills.

Example: I would like to read about how I can burn more calories when I walk, and I would like to meet with a trainer so that he or she can show me how to do the best warm-up and cool-down to avoid injury.

What I need to know to do this task with confidence:

. . . .

Do I know all these things?   Yes/No

If yes, brilliant! Move on to the next section. If no, group the identified gaps in your information or skill base into these categories:

To ask someone about:

. . . .

To read about:

. . . .

To take a course about:

. . . .

To engage a coach or trainer who could teach me:

. . . .

To hire a professional who could do this for me:

. . . .

Then practice the routine we've established: For any of the items that fall into the *To . . .* category, I want you to identify the action steps and put a time in your calendar when you can move forward on them. As always, you can use the "Simple Project Plan" template to get your thoughts organized on paper.

Congrats! You've laid the foundation. Now it's time to script the actual routine.

Step 2: Anticipate Everything

Set Realistic Expectations

As explained in Chapter 5, a huge component of your emotional state and overall happiness with life revolves around your ability to set realistic expectations about how long it takes you to get things done, how much time you have to invest each day, and the way that you actually work versus the way that you think or feel you should work.

Once you've clarified the action that you would like to take, such as walk outside for 20 minutes each morning, I want you to put it through these expectations cross-checks:

- **How much time do I need to set aside for this activity? Example:** If I'm going to walk for 20 minutes, I need to set aside about 5 to 10 minutes beforehand to change my clothes and put on my shoes and, if necessary, a coat, gloves, and a scarf. After I walk, I'll need to take a few minutes to stretch before I get ready for the day. This means that for 20 minutes of walking, I need to allocate 30 to 40 minutes of my morning.
- **Do I have the free space to invest in this activity? Example:** On most mornings, I can invest 30 to 40 minutes without a problem, but on Wednesdays, I have an 8 a.m. meeting, so exercising would be tough. I can't really fit in a walk on Wednesday morning without major stress.
- **Am I a moderator or an abstainer?** You will want to set your goals based on what you find most motivating for change. If you're a moderator, you will be more content and feel less restricted by having this type of expectation: I will go on a morning walk three to four times a week. If you have more of an all-or-nothing attitude, you will tend to find this approach more freeing: I will go on a 20-minute walk every morning except Wednesday, when I have an 8 a.m. meeting.

I need this much time:

. . . .

Do I have this time?   Yes/No

How often will I do this activity?

. . . .

Plan Your Warm-Up

Now it's time to plan your approach. Ignoring what leads up to performing a certain action is one of the *biggest* reasons that people have failed launches of new routines, so . . . pay close attention to this part.

I want you to start to think through what needs to happen and what you need to avoid earlier that day or even in prior days in order to be ready for action when the designated time comes.

Example: If I am going to exercise for 20 minutes each morning, I need to start getting ready for bed around 10 p.m. This means shutting down my computer and not taking any calls from people who will want to have an extended conversation with me after that time. It also means going around the house and putting away anything that might distract me in the morning, such as dirty dishes or random mail. Before I go to bed, I will either put on my exercise clothes or lay them out at the foot of my bed. I will also put out my walking shoes and water bottle. By 11 p.m., I need to stop reading and have lights-out time. As soon as I get up, I need to immediately put on my shoes, grab my water bottle, and head outside before anything else distracts me.

Now consider what will need to happen leading up to the start of your main action.

What will I need to prepare?

. . . .

What limits will I need to set on my time? On my activities? On other people?

. . . .

How can I make the process as smooth and frictionless as possible?

. . . .

Pick a Start Time or Trigger

To lower the force required to break inertia and to build momentum, pick a start time or trigger event. This keeps you from having to make (and remake) the decision of whether this activity stands as your highest priority in the moment. It also takes away any lack of clarity about how and when the routine will fit into your schedule, which helps with realistic expectations. Without a start time or trigger, you can come to the end of the day, fall into bed, and realize that you never moved ahead on what you planned to do.

Example of a start time: I will begin putting on my shoes and head out of the door around 6:30 a.m.

Example of a start trigger: After I take out the dogs, put water in their bowls, and start the coffee pot, I will begin putting on my shoes and head out of the door.

Either system can work, but to decide which one suits your routine best, consider these points:

- **Start times work well when you have a high level of control over your schedule.** They also are sometimes necessary if you have a set limit on your end time, such as needing to arrive at work at a certain time.
- **Start triggers work well if you have some variables outside your control**, which means that your life can't run on clockwork precision. Also, in order for start triggers to be effective, they *must* happen every time you want to start on your routine.

My start time or trigger is:

. . . .

Define the Very First Step

To make your routines as easy as possible to start and to implement consistently, the first step should seem so small, so simple, so elementary that you can't help but take it with confidence, which leads you to the next step and the next one and the next one. Right now, I want you to visualize that very first step that will lead you down the path of your new routine. What will it look like? What will it feel like?

Example visualization: I'll pull back the sheets on my bed so that they form a crumpled triangle over the top of my comforter. Then I'll shuffle across the room, lift up my mobile phone, and turn off the alarm. I'll yawn a bit as I shuffle back toward my bed—but not allow myself to lie down again—instead, I'll perch on its edge, put on my right shoe, lace it up, and then put on my left shoe and lace it up. I'll get up slowly so that I don't give myself a headache. Then I'll stretch my arms up high above my head,

reaching my hands up to the ceiling to get some oxygen and energy flowing. Then I'll stretch my neck to the left and to the right and walk out of my room and down the stairs.

This exercise helps you to focus on the first step—getting out of bed and putting on your shoes—instead of the big picture goal of walking for 20 minutes. By giving your mind something extremely nonthreatening and doable, you dramatically decrease barriers to action and make the "directions" extremely clear.

My very first step will look like:

. . . .

Rethink Unhelpful Mental Patterns

After Chapters 2 and 3, you should have ninja-level skills at shifting your mind-set, so we won't go in depth into how to do that here. But I do want you to anticipate any mental patterns or emotional triggers that may work against your efforts to implement a routine. Once you identify what may hold you back, you can proactively choose new ways of thinking, which lead to new ways of feeling.

Example of harmful mental patterns: I've never exercised very regularly, so when I think about walking every morning, I feel a sense of anxiety and guilt. Also, these thoughts start to come to mind: I've never been able to exercise consistently, so why should now be any different? I don't want to start because I'm afraid I won't finish. That would be just awful. Not walking every day would prove once again that I'm a failure who can never change.

Example of new, helpful mental patterns: I can give this routine a try and see how it goes. My past does not determine the verdict on my future. I can choose to think differently and act differently, starting now. If I try this routine and it doesn't go exactly as I expected, I will be fine and can choose to adapt the current routine or to try another routine.

When you first start out, you may need to have these new thoughts written out and posted wherever you will take the *very first step*. This

could include putting them on your workspace wall, placing them beside your bed, or putting them on a kitchen cabinet or the refrigerator.

What I'm thinking that creates resistance to this routine:

. . . .

New mental patterns that could put me in a better emotional state and mentally prepare me for action:

. . . .

Acknowledge Any Other Barriers to Success

Even with the best of routines, certain outside factors can have a significant impact on your ability to follow through. In fact, many of these external forces are the very reason that many people resist making and practicing routines. Their logic goes something like this: If I can't implement perfectly and someone might mess up my plans, why even bother?

But the fact that life happens doesn't mean that you should give up all hope of making and following routines. What you can do instead is to anticipate and prepare for potential barriers to success so that they don't keep you from achieving the true priority behind your routines.

Example: If my significant other asks me to start watching a movie anytime after 9:30 p.m., I won't have the ability to turn off the lights by 11 p.m. Also, if it's really cold, rainy, or snowy, I don't feel comfortable walking outside.

These barriers might stand in the way of implementing my routine:

. . . .

Your barriers typically will divide into two groups that require two different types of *anticipation:*

- **Preventable barriers.** These sorts of barriers can throw you off, but they don't need to if you have the right strategy in place. For example,

you could negotiate with your significant other that you won't start watching a movie after 9:30 p.m. If he or she asks anyway, you can plan out what you would say in response to maintain your boundary or compromise by agreeing that you will start preparing for bed around 10:30 p.m., even if the movie hasn't finished.

- **Unpreventable barriers.** Factors such as the weather don't preside within your locus of control. Instead of anticipating how you will prevent them, you need to figure out how to respond so that you still achieve the priority behind your routine even if the path varies. For example, you could come up with an alternate "bad weather exercise routine," where you walk on your treadmill for 20 minutes in the morning instead of walking outside.

How I will avoid preventable barriers:

. . . .

How I will respond to unpreventable barriers:

. . . .

Script What Comes After the Routine

Occasionally, you resist starting a routine because you don't know what you will do after you finish it. This apprehension about what's next can reduce the ease with which you carry out simple daily routines. This approach avoidance occurs most strongly when the desired new routine will lead you to a place where you feel uncomfortable or unfamiliar or face the potential for judgment. For example, an artist may fear facing critiques after she regularly spends time on a painting and actually completes it, or a job applicant may feel uncertain about what he will do once he's asked to have an interview. This is why you want to have at least a rough idea of what's next so that your subconscious doesn't fear finishing.

Example: Following my morning walk, I will drink a cup of coffee, get into the shower, and then get ready to leave.

More complex example: Following the completion of my artwork, I will visit two galleries each week to find out whether they might put my work on display in their space.

I will do this following the completion of my routine:

. . . .

Step 3: Practice the Routine

Now is the time to do what you just planned in step 2. Treat this process as an experiment where success means attempting to do what you planned, not flawless execution. It's okay—normal in fact—to feel silly, awkward, or downright bad at this stage. Just like a child learning to walk, you need to toddle before you can run.

I will start practicing the routine at this time and on this day:

. . . .

Step 4: Review, Reward, and Recalibrate

Track Your Progress

When you don't have some sort of external marker of what you've done or haven't done, your results can get really foggy in your mind. This also can make it extremely difficult to review and reflect on what has worked or hasn't worked. This is why some sort of tracking system can make sticking to a routine easier.

Examples for tracking days of walking:

- Make an X on the calendar.
- Draw a hash mark on my weekly to-do list.
- Move a pebble from one tray to the next.
- Check it off my daily online to-do list.

- Place a sticker on a chart.
- Tell someone I see daily when I've done my walk.

I will track my progress by:

....

I will be accountable to this person:

....

Celebrate Incremental Improvements

Strengthening new routines is hard work, so you need to be super encouraging of yourself each step of the way. I want you to evaluate your progress on regular intervals based on time-bound reminders or action-related triggers (e.g., once a week or at the end of each time you complete a specific routine).

Your review should begin with focusing on the positive: what went right, what's better than you did before, and how you responded well. By choosing to emphasize your improvements—almost to the point of hyperbole—you build momentum for future success.

Example: I went on a walk twice this week. That was 200 percent more than I have done in the last six months. I'm really proud of that improvement. I would like to work toward exercising almost every day. So when I reach two weeks in a row where I walk five times each week, I will treat myself to downloading two new books and a few songs.

I will congratulate myself for incremental improvement by:

....

I will reward myself for reaching a larger goal by:

....

Refine and Recalibrate

Although you should feel really proud of every little bit of progress, it's completely acceptable and good to refine and recalibrate your routines.

Here's the secret to critiquing the results without becoming self-critical: You want total emotional engagement in celebrating your successes, but when you refine and recalibrate, your goal should be dispassionate analysis of the "experiment" that is your routine. This mind-set helps you to examine the results of practicing the routine without making you feel inadequate or like a failure as a person.

Example: I noticed that when I bring the dogs out on a leash, they are ready to come back in much sooner than when I just let them run free in the yard. I think I'll take them out on a leash on weekday mornings so that I can start my walk earlier. I also noticed that I am much more comfortable and more likely to head out the door when I wear a few extra layers. I'm going to bundle up more before going outside on cold days.

Ask yourself these kinds of questions during the evaluation process:

- Do any parts of this routine cause me frustration or slow me down?
- Do I have negative associations with any element of the routine?
- Could I make part of my routine easier by adjusting the time or my methods?
- Could I think differently about this routine to make it easier for me to do?
- Even if I can't complete the entire routine, how can I ensure that I still accomplish my underlying goal?

Way to go! You've gone through the process of developing your own custom routine. I'm so proud of you. You can take advantage of the "Create Your Own Routine" and "Simple Project Plan" templates to implement this process again and again. In the coming pages, you'll also see sample real-life routines that you can modify to suit your needs.

Create Your Own Routine Template

(You can download a digital copy at www.reallifee.com/tib.)

Special note: Use as much or as little of these steps as you find helpful to develop and strengthen your routines.

Step 1: Prepare for Action

My priority area is:

....

I prefer this approach to change:

....

I will take this action:

....

Then put the equipment and supplies into these categories:
Ready to go: ....
To buy: ....
To borrow: ....
To find: ....
To clean: ....
To prepare: ....

My ideal environment is:
What I need to find: ....
What I need to create or build: ....
What I need to change: ....
What I need to clean: ....
What I need to eliminate: ....
What I need to communicate to others who
      share the space: ....

What do I need to know to do this task with confidence?

....

Do I know all these things?   Yes/No

If no:

To ask someone about: ....

To read about: ....

To take a course about: ....

To engage a coach or trainer who could teach me: ....

To hire a professional who could do this for me: ....

Step 2: Anticipate Everything

I need this much time:

....

Do I have this time?   Yes/No

How often will I do this activity?

....

What will I need to prepare?

....

What limits will I need to set on my time? On my activities? On other people?

....

How can I make the process as smooth and frictionless as possible?

....

My start time or trigger is:

....

My very first step will look like:

. . . .

What I'm thinking that creates resistance to this routine:

. . . .

New mental patterns that could put me in a better emotional state and mentally prepare me for action:

. . . .

These barriers might stand in the way of implementing my routine:

. . . .

How I will avoid preventable barriers:

. . . .

How I will respond to unpreventable barriers:

. . . .

I will do this following completion of my routine:

. . . .

Step 3: Practice the Routine

I will start practicing the routine on this time and day:

. . . .

Step 4: Review, Reward, and Recalibrate

I will track my progress by:

....

I will be accountable to this person:

....

I will congratulate myself for incremental improvement by:

....

I will reward myself for reaching a larger goal by:

....

Do any parts of this routine cause me frustration or slow me down?

....

Do I have negative associations with any element of the routine?

....

Could I make part of my routine easier by adjusting the time or my methods?

....

Could I think differently about this routine to make it easier for me to do?

....

Even if I can't complete the entire routine, how can I ensure that I still accomplish my underlying goal?

. . . .

Simple Project Plan Template

(You can download a digital copy at www.reallifee.com/tib.)

What result do I desire?

. . . .

What actions do I need to do to achieve that result?

. . . .

. . . .

Does it matter in which order I complete the steps?   *Yes/No*

If yes, number the preceding actions in priority order or at least group them together so that you have a rough sense of the progression.

Write a rough estimate of the completion time beside each of the preceding action steps.

Put time in your schedule to move forward on the action steps. Or if you have a fixed deadline that you need to meet, block in time for all the activities between now and the deadline so that you know how to pace yourself.

Quick Reference Done-for-You Routines and Tools

- Planning routines
  - Sunday evening weekly planning and daily morning planning
  - Monday afternoon weekly planning
  - Wednesday-to-Wednesday review
  - Friday morning weekly planning and processing
  - Daily routine
  - Daily wrap-up
  - To-do list tools
- Project completion routines
  - Deciding whether to take on new projects
  - Turning projects into action plans
  - Zooming in to avoid overwhelm
  - Eliminating deadline stress
  - Rewarding efficiency to prevent resentment
  - Project organization tools
- E-mail processing routines
  - Clearing your inboxes efficiently
  - Extracting to-do items from e-mail
  - Consistently feeling on top of e-mail
  - E-mail tools
- Work and school routines
  - Determining optimal work hours
  - Running efficient meetings
  - Making a good impression at meetings
  - Leading effectively in contentious meetings
  - Staying balanced during business travel
  - Studying for the Graduate Record Exam (GRE)
  - Fitting class work around a full-time job
  - Virtual meeting tools
- Mental decompression routines
  - Simple morning meditation
  - Evening praise time
  - Afternoon breaks
  - Forgiving myself

- Relaxation tools
- Sleep, food, and exercise routines
  - Shifting to an earlier schedule
  - Getting to bed on time
  - Meal and grocery planning
  - Healthy eating out and at home
  - Morning cardio
  - Physical therapy exercises
  - Health tools
- Relationship routines
  - Making weekly social plans
  - Keeping in touch long distance
  - Maintaining friendships
  - Relationship-building tools
- Home routines
  - Daily tidying
  - Car cleaning
  - Lunchtime reading
  - Office organization
  - Bill payment
  - Child's school schedule
  - Home tools

Planning Routines

Sunday Evening Weekly Planning and Daily Morning Planning

Current Status

- Conflict
  - Intellectually: Seems like a good idea.
  - Emotionally: Seems like a waste of time.
- Good associations with planning when:
  - I get everything done on my list.
  - It helps me anticipate items.
  - I feel I used all my time well.

Daily Planning Routine

- Monday through Friday at 9 a.m.
- Items needed:
  - Google calendar
    - Calendar items
    - Calendar reminders
  - Weekly to-do list (print out)
- Make daily to-do list on a Post-it.

Weekly Planning Routine

- Sunday
- Items needed:
  - Priority checklist
  - Monthly or long-term list
  - Project to-do list (Post-it note)
    - In the future: Folder for every project that I work on with the planning sheet.
  - Lists:
    - Blog post ideas
    - Groceries
- Review the preceding lists and decide whether to:
  - Plan an activity for the week based on these lists.
  - And/or add a to-do item to your weekly to-do list.

Points to Keep in Mind

- Planning is not meant to limit you but to give you the satisfaction that you're using your time well.
- Your schedule is your servant, not your master.

DAY IN THE LIFE OF A TIME COACH

For an in-depth look at my morning planning and processing routine, go to www.reallifee.com/day-in-the-life-of-a-time-coach-my-planning-routine.

Monday Afternoon Weekly Planning

Current Method

- When you feel a sense of urgency, you make a daily to-do list.

Ideal Method

- Each Monday when you get your Starbucks schedule, you can then sketch in when you would like to move forward on these activities:
  - Starbucks hours
  - Physical therapy, doctors' appointments, church, etc.
  - Prayer time
  - Daily processing—calls, e-mails, etc.
  - Important goals for the week
  - Errands
  - Grocery shopping
  - Exercise
  - Physical therapy exercises
  - Friends and family time
  - Creative project

Each morning, you can then look at the day's main activities and make adjustments for changes from the prior day.

Why This Is Ideal

- This routine will give you time to accomplish more.
- You'll be able to do extra things that you haven't been able to do.
- You'll not be frustrated and disappointed with yourself.

A Few Final Points

- The key to your dream of a peaceful, productive day is not a secret—not a black box. This is something you can attain by following these strategies.

- It's a good idea to put in some extra goals for the week that give you energy and stretch you to see how much you are capable of accomplishing.
- It's a great idea to keep two lists: weekly to-dos and someday/maybe items so that they're off your mind and available for weekly planning.

Wednesday-to-Wednesday Review

Weekly Review

- Two to two-and-a-half hours on Tuesday mornings
- 7:00 to 9:30 a.m.
  - Clean up the past week:
    - Clean desk.
    - File papers.
    - Follow up e-mail folder.
    - Close out files.
    - Inbox to zero.
    - Have a plan for deliverables such as reviewing documents before a meeting.
    - Revisit your follow-up list:
      - Make a plan to address items.
      - Get rid of what you have addressed.
    - Know what you need to do personally to be ready.
    - Schedule in and out time.
    - Look at priority checklist.

What Has Stood in the Way in the Past

- Feeling like it's a luxury I couldn't afford
- Feeling so behind on deadline-driven items
- Feeling like I don't have the time
- Wondering what my coworkers would think of me:
  - Probably more of a feeling than a reality
  - Boss tells me to go home and leave on Fridays

Why This Is Important

- Makes my whole week less reactionary
- Reduces my stress
- Makes me look like my world is together
- Helps me save face
- I find it very refreshing.
- It's a nice mental break.

What You Can Do

- Put weekly review on the white board.
- Tell yourself:
  - Next week's weekly review will take twice as long if I skip a week.
  - It's not a luxury.
  - This helps me be more efficient.

Points to Keep in Mind

- Planning is not meant to limit you but to give you the satisfaction that you're using your time well.
- Your schedule is your servant, not your master.
- You'll also want to put in a time to look at what's coming up personally and professionally—forward perspective.

LEARN FROM A MASTER

David Allen provides in-depth instructions on planning routines in his iconic book *Getting Things Done* (New York: Viking Penguin, 2001). Check it out for actionable ideas.

Friday Morning Weekly Planning and Processing

Highest Priorities

- Half-hour processing, one hour reviewing next actions, half-hour time blocking

- Be clear on what's most critical, and plan time for it in the coming week.
- Remind yourself that you can't do everything that's important all at once.

Set Aside Two Hours on Friday Mornings For

- Processing next action list: printing it out, starring important, deleting completed
- Setting priorities
- Processing index card stack
- Time blocking next week
- Scheduling interviews
- Strategizing how to use small blocks of time: processing index cards, e-mail, voicemail, etc.
- Planning when to complete longer projects
- Blocking out Friday afternoon for pre-weekend wrap-up
- Answering voicemail
- Answering urgent e-mails

Keep in Mind

- I am planning not doing.
- Everything needs to get done, but it doesn't need to be done now.

Daily Routine

Why this is helpful: You do best having a linear progression of tasks and having a large block of time to focus on a single type of activity.

- **First 15 to 20 minutes:** Quick e-mail check and daily to-do list at a coffee area
- **Next three to four hours:** Focus on specific quality work that you decided was a priority during your week review. This could also be a time to meet with clients.
- **Lunch break**
- **Next one hour:** E-mail inbox to zero

- **Quick:**
  - Update master spreadsheet.
  - Send boss an update.
  - If necessary, check in with the person working for you.
- **Next two to three hours:** Take care of fire drills, administrative work, and follow up.
- **Around 5 or 6 p.m.:**
  - Assess what must be done before you leave the office and begin wrap-up.
  - Celebrate what you were able to accomplish and what you did well.
- **Friday after dinner:** Personal planning
  - Weekend schedule: What can I do that will reenergize me?
  - Fitness schedule
  - Go grocery shopping or plan to go on Saturday morning.
- **Reminder of mental affirmations:**
  - Despite my external circumstances, I can feel an internal sense of peace, calm, and control.
  - I can create a greater sense of control by slowing down and planning what I will do instead of simply reacting to whatever comes my way.
  - By completing the most important work first, I will feel a greater sense of accomplishment and fulfillment in my work.
  - I need to face things head on and look beyond the day to gain perspective.

Daily Wrap-Up

Each Day

- Set an alarm for 45 minutes before I want to leave.
- Spend the last 15 to 30 minutes at my desk.
- Do a quick e-mail check and review these documents:
  - Master to-do list
  - Priorities document
  - Calendar
  - Team to-do list
  - Daily to-do list

    ◦ Task list in Outlook (once or twice a day, move to your master to-do list)
- Look at tomorrow:
  - Decide on my in and out times.
  - Set in an out basket whatever I need for tomorrow's meetings.
  - Capture any new items.
  - Look through notebook with meeting notes.
  - Clean and tidy surfaces.

Why This Is Worthwhile

- Daily processing gives you an internal sense of control and perspective.
- This allows you to feel like a captain of your life instead of being blown around by the winds of change around you.

To-Do List Tools

- **Evernote (www.evernote.com).** Keep all the bits and pieces of your life in one place that is easy to access—from notes to photos to files to web clips to audio recordings.
- **Remember The Milk (www.rememberthemilk.com).** Manage your tasks online or offline and receive e-mail, SMS, or IM reminders.
- **TeuxDeux (www.teuxdeux.com).** Simple, beautiful to-do app. Enough said.
- **Wunderlist (www.wunderlist.com).** Come up with task lists that you can check through your mobile device, computer, or web browser. Also share tasks and lists with others through e-mail.
- **Springpad (www.springpad.com).** Create online notebooks with ideas, photos, barcodes, audio notes, maps, etc., and invite others to participate in specific notebooks. View the information as a project board diagram.

Project-Completion Routines

Deciding Whether to Take on New Projects

Goal

- Clarity on what you will truly commit to or let go
- Confidence about future decisions, whether you can say yes or no

Write Down Your Projects in This Format

- Main project:
  - Cost: Number of hours or days
  - Action steps

Look at Open Blocks of Time in Your Schedule

- Do you have enough time to cover the cost of all the activities?
- If you have enough time, block them all in, and proceed accordingly.
- If you don't have enough time, decide what you will not do or not do until a later date.
- Try to not take on any new projects until some of the current ones are done.

Turning Projects into Action Plans

Goal

- To clarify the required action steps within a short amount of time after accepting a new project.

To Make an Action Plan

- Write out everything involved in completing the project.
- Make a rough estimate of how long you think it will take you to complete the elements of the project. Then add in some "extra" time for the unexpected.
- Take note of any important deadlines.
- Ideally, work backward from the deadline to the present, blocking in when you will spend time on this task. At minimum, set a certain date when you will start on the first actions that need to be completed.
- During your weekly planning, review this action plan to determine what are the best next actions.

Zooming in to Avoid Overwhelm

- **Decide on one measurable action step that you can do each day.** This could include such items as spending 30 minutes completing

a job application or saying one nice thing to the other person in a strained relationship.

- **Come up with a system of recording your action steps in a clear, easy manner.** For instance, this could include a weekly checklist or a series of star stickers or getting to cross out a recurring task on your calendar.
- **Whenever you do what you intended, celebrate big time!** I am serious. Throw your fist in the air, look in the mirror, and tell your reflection, "I'm awesome," or do whatever else you like to do to give yourself a huge energy boost.
- **Whenever action steps don't go as you expected, turn off your emotions, and pretend you're an archeologist or a detective investigating a site.** Observe the who, what, where, why, when, and how of what happened or didn't happen, and then ask yourself, "What can I do differently next time so that I complete the desired action steps?"
- **Repeat daily.**
- **On a less frequent basis, such as once a week or once a month, you should measure your desired results.** The best way to remember to take this action without thinking about it all the time is to put it as a repeat reminder on your calendar.
- **If you see any progress in the right direction, celebrate like you just made the winning touchdown!** It doesn't matter if the scale measures 0.2 pound less or you simply saw your boss smile at you for the first time in a month, chalk it up as progress and success in the making.
- **If you don't see progress in the right direction, you'll experience the temptation to feel frustrated, defiant, angry, or even betrayed.** I did what I was supposed to do! Why didn't it work? Once again, it's time to have an out-of-body experience. Step back, observe, and learn from the past. Decide if you could or should do anything differently in the future or if you simply need to keep at your current action steps. If you can't figure out what could be different, ask a true outside observer for his or her feedback.
- **Make the most recent measured result your new starting point (regardless of whether it is an improvement on the previous measurement) and then measure your following progress from there.**
- **Repeat regularly.**

> **DELEGATE FIRST**
>
> The very first time you see a new task or receive a new project, ask yourself, "Am I the best person for this activity, or could I delegate part or all of it?"

Eliminating Deadline Stress

Strategy

- Give yourself a personal deadline to complete the project the day before it's due so that you always have a buffer.
- Calibrate your schedule to your unique style of work.

Why?

- This will make me happy.
- This will be less stressful.
- I'm doing this for myself.
- When I wait until the last minute, I end up spending so much more time and sometimes more money.
- When I meet my own personal deadline, I'll spend less time and less money.
- I'll have more of a sense of control.
- I'll feel more empowered instead of a slave to the time.
- I'm choosing to do this now.

Rewarding Efficiency to Prevent Resentment

Instead of Just Working More, Do This:

- Tell yourself, "As soon as I get _____ done, then I can _____."
  - **Why?** With this approach, there is not just more work if you're efficient. There's a reward for working quicker.
- Give yourself an end time, and stop working no matter how much you have gotten done during the day.

> - **Why?** This lessens the tendency to procrastinate because of the thought that you could just work later.
- Give yourself one day a week off.
  - **Why?** You feel so much happier about life.

Project Organization Tools

- **Harvest (www.getharvest.com).** Simple time-tracking tool that allows for easier recording of team members' time and faster, more accurate estimates.
- **iDoneThis (www.idonethis.com).** Each evening, an e-mail goes out to everyone asking them to reply with what they've completed. Each morning, all team members receive an e-mail with the compiled digest of updates.
- **Google docs (www.docs.google.com).** Share and edit documents, forms, spreadsheets, and PowerPoint files with other invited collaborators.
- **Basecamp (www.basecamp.com).** A project collaboration tool to share files, develop action steps, and set deadlines. Save framework designs and standardized checklists that you can reuse on similar projects.
- **Asana (www.asana.com).** Divide different areas of your life into "workspaces" with teams, people, and their tasks organized within each one. Stay informed of changes to the tasks and see the task history.
- **15Five (www.15five.com).** This simple feedback system has employees complete weekly reports in 15 minutes or less that their managers can review in five minutes or less and then pass on as meaningful reports to the CEO.

E-mail Processing Routines

Clearing Your Inboxes Efficiently

- **If you have set the expectation that you will respond to e-mails in two seconds flat, set up an autoresponder to start to wean people off of instant access to you.** You want to establish the new expectation that you will only reply to e-mails once or twice a day.

- **Set aside a day to completely clear out your inboxes.** This could be shorter or longer depending on your backlog.
- **At the designated time, sit down with a list of all your e-mail accounts in front of you.** Number them in order of attack.
- **Look at the first inbox.** Select and delete all the messages that do not require a personal response (e.g., updates, newsletters, feeds, list serves, etc.). If you can't bear the thought of deleting something because you "will read it," move it into a properly labeled e-mail folder.
- **Select and move all the e-mails related to a particular project/person/topic that you need to keep but don't require a reply into designated folders.**
- **Take a hard look at your inbox and make sure there is nothing more you can delete or file before starting to read e-mail.**
- **Click on the first message in your inbox.** Take the appropriate action (i.e., read, reply, forward, etc.), and then immediately delete or file it. If you need to remember to complete a task related to that e-mail, put a note on your to-do list or calendar, and then file the e-mail.
- **Continue down the list of e-mails until you are done with the inbox.** The only time you should scan the entire inbox is if you can respond to multiple messages in a conversation thread with a single e-mail.
- **Repeat this process with the rest of your e-mail inboxes.** The psychological relief will be sublime!
- **Develop a personal system of responding to e-mails just once or twice a day so that you can stay on top of e-mail on a regular basis without having it constantly interrupt you.**

A TIME COACH'S APPROACH TO E-MAIL

I block out one to two hours every morning to clear out my e-mails, voicemail, and paper notes and to go through my project lists, calendar, and social media channels. Then, for the rest of the day, I am free to complete projects. I send e-mails as necessary but try to scan my inbox only a couple of times a day and only respond to e-mails that are truly urgent. Otherwise, they have to wait for my morning e-mail purge. I've let clients know that if they need an immediate response they should put "Urgent" in the subject line.

Extracting To-Do Items from E-mail

Action Strategies

- Work on e-mail right after your planning time.
- Mark as unread and flag e-mails to which you need to respond.
- Send a quick reply saying that you received the e-mail and are working on getting the information when you don't know the answer immediately.
- Set a reminder to follow up on any information you request from others.
- With a longer e-mail:
  - Make a new task.
  - Break down the action steps in the notes section.
  - Put in a due date as a reminder to follow up on missing information.

To Make Sure You Have a Complete Capture

- During daily planning, go through all your input areas, that is, iCal, paper, phone, etc.
- Text yourself a reminder or immediately put a task on your calendar.
- If people ask you for something on the fly, ask them to follow up with a request via e-mail.

Consistently Feeling on Top of E-mail

Current Status

- Huge fluctuation—inbox to empty—up to 20 pages
- It tends to manage me.
- I don't schedule time for it, so it gets done on the in-betweens or early in the morning or late at night.
- I have weeks when I didn't accomplish any of my goals because I was answering e-mails.
- Default work when not in a meeting
- Easier than having to do thinking work

Relationship with E-mail

- Love-hate
- Want to be responsive
- Makes me feel a sense of satisfaction and accomplishment to complete
- My e-mail inbox will get ridiculous, so I'll tear into it and then think that it will be under control. Then I let it go (binge-diet approach).

How Important Is Answering E-mail?

- Critical e-mails where I'm slowing work down are important.
- Other e-mails are not as important.

Time to Set Aside for E-mail

- Ninety minutes set aside for e-mail
- Makes me feel like I might be able to stay up on it
- Feel hopeful

Potential System

- Two blocks of 45 minutes
- Before lunch and at the end of the day
- Set timers if you find it to be helpful.
- Turn longer replies into to-do items.
- Decide that your "what's most important now" list is your default between meetings, not e-mail.

Most Important Points

- E-mail takes time.

AUTHOR OF *18 MINUTES* ON E-MAIL

Check out Peter Bregman's "Super-Efficient E-mail Process" at http://blogs.hbr.org/bregman/2012/05/a-super-efficient -email-proces.html.

- My "what's most important now" document is my default.
- Most e-mails aren't urgent.
- I need to make a decision on what to do with the e-mail immediately, and be consistent in my process.

E-mail Tools

- **Boomerang (www.baydin.com).** Schedule e-mails to send at a designated time, have e-mails return to the top of your inbox when you need them, and receive reminders to follow up on important e-mails.
- **AwayFind (www.awayfind.com).** Receive a text message, a voice call, or an alert from a mobile app when you receive an urgent e-mail from an important person or about an important topic so that you don't need to constantly check your inbox.
- **SaneBox (www.sanebox.com).** Algorithms filter your inbox, moving unimportant messages into a separate folder and summarizing them for you.

Work and School Routines

Determining Optimal Work Hours

Ask Yourself These Questions

- What number of hours would I like to work in order to fulfill my job responsibilities and/or run my business?
- Does this leave any time for the other activities I enjoy and for self-care?
- When do I have the most energy?
- Am I most productive in the morning or at night?
- Are there particular days when I'm able to work more or less (e.g., I may be more motivated on Mondays or have a special activity on Thursdays)?
- Do I perform better working straight through lunch, or do I function better when I take a break?

Running Efficient Meetings

One Week Before a Meeting

- Have an agenda sent beforehand (may be able to delegate or use a standard template).
- If there's a decision to be made or information to be covered:
  - Delegate the assignments.
  - Bring the information and/or make the alternatives clear.

During the Meeting

- Set the tone that you want the meeting to take the right amount of time.
- Clearly introduce the meeting by explaining:
  - You understand that everyone's time is valuable.
  - Meetings are done when:
    - The prioritized items are addressed.
    - We have a decision.
    - We have defined next steps in terms of action, owner, and a time frame.
  - Topics will be kept to a certain amount of time.
  - Unrelated topics will need to be discussed through another channel or at a later meeting.
  - Next actions will be assigned.
- Each meeting, time-box the topics. (**Example:** When we get to 10 minutes on a topic, we'll do a time check and then potentially move on.)

After the Meeting

- Follow up on next actions in your one-on-one discussions.

Why This Is Important

- This is the best use of everyone's time.
- I want to set urgency around meetings so that we can do more with less.
- I want the whole team to be more productive and satisfied.

- I want to lead by example of doing this well.
- I want to be a role model and also leverage other people's strengths.

Making a Good Impression at Meetings

- As part of your morning planning, allocate time before a meeting to:
  - Review documents.
  - If necessary, contact the meeting organizer or confer with colleagues.
  - Prepare a few discussion points.
  - Reflect on the points.
- During the meeting:
  - Stay engaged in the conversation.
  - Give good direction.
  - Refer to previous examples.
  - Impart calmness and let them know that you'll work on solutions together.
- After the meeting:
  - Send the organizer a summary of key points.
  - Send an e-mail to senior people saying that you're happy to take the lead on finding a solution.
  - Comment on the minutes.
  - Put quick notes in your task list.

Points to Keep in Mind

- You don't need to change your personality.
- You can make small adaptations to your behavior to amplify the impact of what you're already doing.
- Making these tasks a priority will mean having to say "No" sometimes.

Leading Effectively in Contentious Meetings

Before Each Meeting

- Think through objectives.

- Decide on primary task-oriented deliverables, such as:
  - Coming to a decision
  - Brainstorming a solution to a problem
  - Communicating progress updates
- Come up with at least one relationship-oriented objective, such as:
  - Affirming a colleague in his or her ability
  - Better understanding someone's perspective

During Each Meeting

- Consistently set expectations
- Start each meeting you facilitate with a similar intro, explaining:
  - What you would like to accomplish to put the goal line in place
  - Why you want to accomplish it to give the focus a purpose
  - Make it clear that your increased control isn't about your having a power trip or your being angry but about your having a clear perspective on how the team needs to advance in order to reach your end goal on time.
  - You can also explain that you'll pull them back in if they get off track, but that you are happy for them to share their ideas with you through e-mail as potential topics for an upcoming meeting.

Keep It Fun

Try to think of a light-hearted way to let people know that they're getting off track. It could be something like saying, "I think I just heard a splash," meaning we lost focus from our key objectives, and you fell off the surf board. Or you could toss a starfish-shaped pad of sticky notes to someone who gets off topic as a reminder that he or she should write down divergent thoughts and hand them to you at the end of the meeting. I know that these can sound a bit corny, but they engage the team in moving toward an increased sense of control and focus.

Assess After Each Meeting

- As you're walking away from a meeting, try to ask yourself:
  - Did I clearly explain our current status, what we need to accomplish, and why we need to accomplish it to reach our end destination?

- Did we accomplish our tangible meeting goals?
- Did I make progress on my intangible meeting goals?
- Did I build the relationships?
- What went right?

> **LEAVING TOWN?**
>
> Find a comprehensive travel check list at www.reallifee.com/comprehensive-travel-check-list-for-preparing-for-a-trip.

Staying Balanced During Business Travel

Key Objectives

- Diet
- Exercise
- Staying caught up on e-mails
- Keeping in touch with my direct reports
- Communicating with my family
- Book to read
- One project
- Weekly review

Diet Strategy

- Don't snack, and watch how much I eat at meals.
- Drink water.
- Stay focused on talking with people during breaks.

Exercise Strategy

- Make sure that I pack something that's easy to throw on and go.
- First thing when I get up in the morning, I should go on a walk.
- Prepare ahead of time so that I'm not doing morning catch-up.

E-mail Strategy

- E-mail—30 minutes in the morning

- E-mail—30 minutes around lunch
- E-mail—30 minutes in the evening
- Catch up on e-mail on the airplane or at the airport.
- Set aside the time.
- Give myself freedom to talk to people when it's not e-mail time.

Keeping in Touch with My Direct Reports

- Quick e-mail at the beginning of the day:
  - Highlights from the meeting
  - Let people know about anything special in their specific topic areas.
- Make a quick call or text message to key people.

Keeping in Touch with Family

- Text my wife a few times during the day.
- Call my wife before dinner and before bedtime.
- Text the kids.

Other Areas

- Pick one book, and take it.
- Pick one project, and bring materials.
- Do weekly planning on the plane ride home.

Studying for the Graduate Record Exam (GRE)

Mental Prep

- Decide that you want to study for the GRE:
  - I know that this is something that I need to do and ultimately what I want to do.
  - In order to be in grad school and finish, this is the first step.
  - Once I get this unlocked, I can pretty much do anything as far as grad school goes.
  - I want to do this even if I don't feel like doing it.
- Take deep breaths and be present.

- Remember: If I need to, I can take it again.
- Envision: If I get over a _____ on this next GRE, I'll do cartwheels out of the library. I'll be able to do what I want to do and learn what I want to learn.

Schedule

- Plan out specific days and times to move forward on clearly defined activities.

Environmental Prep

- Wean myself off staying focused on food.
- Wear comfortable clothes.
- Bring a snack.

Thinking of the Test as a Game

- I know the answer.
- I can choose which answer is the best.
- The answer is right there.
- The answer is in front of me.

Fitting Class Work Around a Full-Time Job

Mind-set

- Remember that you have nothing to prove.
- You're there to learn and enjoy the process!
- You only need to get a C to be reimbursed.

Time Blocking

- Mondays after dinner: Complete weekly assignment if not done by Sunday evening.
- Tuesdays and Wednesdays after dinner: Hour of catch-up learning.
- Saturdays and Sundays after refreshing and fun activity: Complete assignments.

Bonus Tips

- Aiming to complete assignments by Sunday will dramatically reduce Monday stress.
- Try to set weekly expectations of how many hours you can devote to assignments based on your overall weekly priorities. This will keep you from overspending time on a school assignment at the expense of other more important priorities.

Virtual Meeting Tools

- **Free conference call (www.freeconferencecall.com).** Get a free telephone conference call number so that you can bring together groups of people and have the option to record meetings for later distribution.
- **Google + hangout (www.google.com/+).** See all the conference participants along the bottom of your screen and the current speaker on the top.
- **Skype conference call (www.skype.com).** Make free audio and video conference calls between Skype users anywhere in the world or include phone users for a small fee.
- **GoToMeeting (www.gotomeeting.com).** Use this professional tool for online meetings and webinars complete with invitation tools and post meeting reports.

Mental Decompression Routines

Simple Morning Meditation

When Working from Home

- After taking your dog for a walk, sit for a few minutes in the park and meditate before going home.

When Commuting to the Office

- Listen to guided meditation on your iPad at the beginning of your train ride.

Afternoon Breaks

Strategy

- Put in a weekday reminder at 2 p.m. on your mobile device or computer.
- When it goes off, stretch right away, and get in the mood to take a break and get your lunch.
- Give yourself permission to stop when you're done with the current task.
- **Remember:** I feel tired and have a headache when I don't take a break. I'll have a quick win—but will accomplish less during the day.
- **Remember:** I have everything in my iCal. If I want, I can put to-do items in order so that when I get back from the break, they'll be ready for me.

Forgiving Myself

Release Emotional Drag

- Accept where I am.
- Get my gumption up for giving it my all.
- Forgive myself for:
  - Activities I didn't do
  - Procrastination
  - Undervaluing myself
  - Coasting
  - Being afraid

Relaxation Tools

- **Saagara (www.saagara.com).** Download health tool apps that help you to relax through guided breathing and yoga exercises.
- **Pandora (www.pandora.com).** Listen to relaxation music or whatever else you need to unwind and calm down after a long day on this free Internet radio.

- **Gaiam (www.gaiam.com).** Find products for natural stress relief such as neck and foot massagers.

Sleep, Food, and Exercise Routines

Shifting to an Earlier Schedule

Why This Is Important

- The mornings go much better when you get up and go to bed earlier.
- You feel most centered when you have a consistent sleep routine.

Ideal

- 9 p.m. head to bed
- 10 p.m. go to sleep
- 5 a.m. up for work

Why This Is Difficult

- The whole cycle has to shift.
- It's hard when you've only been home for a few hours.
- Need to leave work earlier at around 4 p.m.
  - Get in around 7 a.m.
  - Takes a shorter time to get home

What Keeps Me at Work

- Lack of internal signal to stop
- The feeling that I could do one more thing
- Only time I can catch my boss
- Tend to get my best work done between 3 and 5 p.m.
- It feels really early when I leave at 4 p.m.

Legitimate Reasons to Stay Later

- Deadlines
- Essential meetings

What Works to Get Out

- Knowing I have to be some place

New Strategy

- Schedule an after-work activity you enjoy.
  - Commitment with friends or family.
  - Appointment or class
- Head to bed around 9 p.m.
  - Install auto-shutdown computer program as a reminder.
  - Put lamp on a timer so that it turns off.
- Spend time knitting
- Go to bed around 10 p.m.
- Alarm at 5 a.m.
  - Do morning ritual.
  - **Why this is important:** You hate the feeling of being rushed in the morning and feeling late to everything.

Getting to Bed on Time

Strategies for Success

- Don't eat or drink after 8 p.m.
- Set alarm to start wind-down around 10 p.m.
- Turn off bright lights.
- Get up and take the dogs outside.
- Turn off the TV or simply leave it off on work nights.
- Brush your teeth, and shut down the computer.
- Read a book.
- Lights out around 11 p.m.

Tell Yourself

- If I go to bed earlier, I'll be able to:
  - Wake up earlier.
  - Take the dogs out earlier.

- Walk the dogs.
- Fit in yoga and meditation with ease.
- Feel better about myself because I'm consistently getting into work on time.
- This is not a punishment.
- I'm doing this for myself to feel more refreshed tomorrow.

Meal and Grocery Planning

Why Plan?

- Logging the food that you're eating and the times you'll be out reduces the emotional component of deciding what to eat and what to buy.
- Meal planning before shopping reduces the need for extra grocery trips.

Sunday Afternoons

- Go through recipes and pick out some that look good to you.
  - Spend 30 minutes to one hour.
  - Choose three or four main courses, including some that are quicker.
- Make a list based on the recipes.
- **Goal:** To be shopping by around 2 p.m.

Daily Basis

- Decide which of the three to four recipes you want to make.
- Have floating days when you don't cook.
- **Goal:** To make cooking and eating dinner as effortless and enjoyable as possible.

Healthy Eating Out and at Home

Each Week

- Plot out the nights you will have dinner out and the nights you're at home.

- For the nights you're eating out, find the menus, and decide what to eat in advance.
- For the nights you're home, plan out healthy meals so that you can get your groceries and other supplies most efficiently.
- A couple of principles that will help:
  - Avoid taking home items that you don't want to eat.
  - Plan on super nutritious, yummy meals that you can look forward to and that will fill you up.
  - Plan on a treat for each day, usually after lunch. If you buy the treats from the grocery store, buy only as much as you would like to eat in the week.

Morning Cardio

Important Mind-set

- Taking time for myself and particularly for exercise is a good and necessary use of my time.
- Exercise plays an important role in maintaining my health and sanity.
- It's worth going to bed and getting up earlier so that I can work out on a more consistent basis.

Action Strategy

- Start to wind down around 8:30 p.m.
  - Wrap up with e-mails.
  - Put away dishes.
  - Get ready for bed.
  - Set out exercise clothes upstairs.
  - Set out water bottle and magazine that you're looking forward to reading downstairs.
- Decide not to start a show that will run past 8:30 p.m.
- Get up at 6 a.m.
- Immediately put on exercise clothes, and go downstairs.
- Go to the gym or do an exercise video in the basement.

A Few More Motivational Thoughts

- It is more important to me to exercise consistently than to spend extra time reading or watching TV at night.
- Following this routine will make me feel like I'm in good shape and able to keep up with the kids.
- This can help with losing a few pounds.
- I will be sore at first, but that's normal, and I will be over that phase soon.
- This is something important that I want to do for my personal health in the short term and is also important long term.
- I'm worth it!

Physical Therapy Exercises

Goal

- To do the exercises every day.

Strategy

- On evenings when you are out at an activity, do the exercises immediately after you get home while listening to music.
- When you spend the evening at home, start on your back exercises at 9 or 9:15 p.m. while you are finishing watching a TV show.

Why This Is Important

- It's the only thing that helps me with not having back pain and headaches.
- Over the long term, it may help my spine to be healthy.

Health Tools

- **Sleepyti.me bedtime calculator (www.sleepyti.me).** Enter the time you need to wake up, and this calculator will tell you what time to go to bed so that you wake up between 90-minute sleep cycles.

- **Pepperplate (www.pepperplate.com).** Import and edit recipes from cooking websites, organize your shopping list, and have the ability to view everything on your mobile device even when offline.
- **FitDay (www.fitday.com).** Use this online diet journal to set goals, track your food, and record your activities.
- **Dailymile (www.dailymile.com).** Track your workouts, and let your friends know about your progress so that they can compete with you or cheer you on or both.

Relationship Routines

Making Weekly Social Plans

Current Status

- When I'm free, I'll call someone.

Ideal

- Want to plan time with people into my schedule so that it's not always last minute or spontaneous
- Want to spend more time with friends and also my sister

To Start

- Would like to have two planned social events a week
- Saturday night and Sunday
- Who would I like to spend time with?
  - List names here:
- Want one of the two events to be a group and the other can be a small group or even one-on-one
- On Friday night, call people to see about the coming weekend.

Keeping in Touch Long Distance

Goal

- To reply within two weeks to personal e-mails by e-mail, text, phone, postcard, or letter

I Have Not Wanted to Respond When

- It is the last thing I want to do at night.
- I associate e-mail with work.
- It seems like an endless task.
- The longer it's been, the less I want to do something because I feel guilty and feel like it needs to be an incredible e-mail.
- I don't feel like I have much to say.
- I don't know exactly how to respond.
- I feel like there's a better use of the time.

I Have Responded to E-mail When

- There's a very specific question I've been asked.
- There are certain people that I want to reply to:
  - There is an expectation that I'll respond.
  - They tend to be short e-mails.
- I can e-mail or call my family on the way to and from work.
- I can call people when I'm on a walk.

I Really Enjoyed Writing Letters and Postcards When

- It was fun.
- I knew fewer people and had fewer competing priorities.
- I put effort into picking interesting stationery and making cards.
- I tended to do this activity on the weekend.

Ideas to Try

- Get a phone card to make less expensive calls.
- Return confusing e-mails with a call or text.
- Use short bits of time on your commute or before work or on lunch break to answer e-mails or text or to make calls (iPhone, home computer, café).
- Send postcards instead of e-mails.
- Move away from all-or-nothing.
  - Write a long e-mail or nothing.
  - Answer all e-mails or nothing.

Feels Good

- Because "layering" activities doesn't feel like a waste of time.
- Keeping up the communication but not spending extra time at the computer, especially on the weekend

Maintaining Friendships

Keeping in Touch with Friends

- Make a list of friends grouped by how frequently you want to connect with them:
  - Weekly
  - Monthly
  - Quarterly
  - Annually
- Schedule a recurring event to meet with people in the various circles at the appropriate frequency or simply set up a next time to meet at the end of the last time you spend with a person.
- Pace your relationships by suggesting dates further out.
- Put a recurring event in your calendar for significant dates such as wedding anniversaries or birthdays.
- Lower your standards for cards and gifts so that you can consistently send an e-mail or e-card instead of waiting for the perfect card or gift and never sending anything at all.

Relationship-Building Tools

- **Smartr (www.xobni.com).** This app creates an automatic address book from all your e-mails and integrates with Facebook, Twitter, and LinkedIn.
- **BirthdayAlarm (www.birthdayalarm.com).** Set up automatic e-mail reminders for birthdays and other special events.
- **Call Your Folks! (www.mokasocial.com/portfolio/call-your-folks/).** You can put recurring reminders in any online calendar to call someone but this Android app makes it more fun to schedule calling Grandma weekly.

- **Hallmark (www.hallmark.com).** Send e-cards for special occasions or just to say hello.

Home Routines

Daily Tidying

After Arriving Home

- Start a load of laundry.
- Set a timer for 30 minutes.
- Focus my attention on my physical environment, and put items in order or away within that time limit.

Car Cleaning

Before Leaving the Car

- Put trash in the garbage can.
- Pick up items to bring in.
- Make multiple trips if necessary so that the car is completely empty after each ride.

Lunchtime Reading

To Read Regularly

- Keep your book by the place where you set your keys when you walk in the door.
- After you drop your keys, pick up the book and bring it with you to wherever you will eat.
- Open it to the correct page so that when you sit down with your lunch, everything is ready and waiting for a few minutes of reading.
- This will help you to make consistent progress and give you time to ponder and apply what you have read.

Office Organization

Vision

- Desktop clear of anything except equipment and decorations
- No random stacks of paper
- No boxes on the floor or stacked paper
- No overflowing inbox of stuff
- Bookshelves purged and organized
- File cabinet purged and maybe new filing space
- Cupboards purged and organized
- Get rid of old computer.
- Implement two-monitor setup.

Materials Needed

- Folders
- Trash cans
- Copy paper box

Process

- Morning—but just do a focused 15 minutes.
- Evening—but just do a focused 15 minutes.

Desktop Order of Organization

- Desk blotter area
- Pile of folders
- Pile of papers on far right
- Papers to the left of the computer

Bill Payment

Best Time

- Between 9 and 11 p.m. on Sunday

Most Common Next Actions

- Bills
  - To make the online payment process effortless:
    - List of all the websites
    - List of the usernames and passwords
    - Keep in a password-protected Excel document or use 1Password (www.agilebits.com/onepassword).
    - **Remember:** Stay focused on getting the payment done. You can go back to look at other things if you still have time and/ or want to spend the time on this task.
    - Average time needed: 30 minutes
  - To make the paper bill payment efficient:
    - Make it a regular Sunday night routine.

Affirmations for Behavioral Change

- I want to get things done and out of my mind so that I have less stress.
- Once this paperwork is done, I can relax.

ROUTINES WITH KIDS

For some great tips on family routines from morning until night, check out this post: www.mightymommy.quickand dirtytips.com/routines-simplify-your-life.aspx.

Child's School Schedule
Kids thrive on routine. Here's how to help your child develop his or her own daily schedule.

Start of Every Day

- Decide on a wake-up time.
  - How do you like to wake up?
  - Do you need "Snooze" or reminders?
- Breakfast
- Clothes for the day

- Make sure that the backpack is packed, including homework and possibly papers that need to be signed.
- Lunch or lunch money and after-school snack
- Do you prefer to shower or bathe in the morning or at night?
- When do you need to leave the house to get to the bus stop?

After-School Routine

- After-school care
- Snack or other food
- Is there homework time or other activities?
- When is the required pickup time?
- Transportation to and from school?

Transitioning Home Routine

- What do you want to do when you get home?
- Do you need space, or do you want to talk?
- Establish rituals with the family.
- Family dinner:
  - Communication and connection
  - Include child in menu planning, cooking, setting the table, putting out water
  - Communicating values and the good of work
- Homework or other studies
- Reading time

Evening Routine

- Thirty-minute cleanup
- Ritual books and reading
- Getting ready for the next day
- Tucking in at night
- Bedtime conversations

Weekend Rituals

- Friday evening movie night
- Saturday breakfast

Home Tools

- **Mint (www.mint.com).** Collect information from all your financial accounts in one place so that you can track your spending, set goals, and make a plan for your best financial decisions.
- **DropBox (www.dropbox.com).** Share large files with others and automatically back up specified files on your computer with this file hosting service.
- **My Job Chart (www.myjobchart.com).** This online program allows kids—and adults—to track their chores and earn points to save, spend, or share.
- **Cozi (www.cozi.com).** Use this online tool to keep an entire family organized, including a shared calendar, shopping lists, to-do lists, family journal, and more.
- **Bookqueue (www.bookqueue.net).** Track your reading, add books to your queue, rate and review books, and if desired, share your log with friends.

CHAPTER 8

BE ACCOUNTABLE

Support for Lasting Change

If you want to go fast, go alone. If you want to go far, go together.

—ANONYMOUS

It Takes a Cheering Squad to Win a Book Contract

Depending on whether you write fiction or nonfiction, you have a different journey to getting a publishing contract. With fiction writing, you need to actually write the entire book (called a *manuscript*) that gets submitted to a publisher. With nonfiction, you write a book proposal first, which is more or less a business plan for your book, and then a publisher decides whether or not to accept your proposal and to pay you an advance on your royalties to write the actual book.

Since this book is an extension of Real Life E Time Coaching and Training's mission of creating a world full of peaceful, confident, and accomplished people, I fell into the nonfiction category. That meant . . . book proposal (ugh.)

Don't get me wrong. I *love* writing, especially about topics that will make a positive difference in people's lives like this book or my many guest posts. But working on the book proposal was really tough for me on a number of fronts. I'm a time coach, and I've trained myself to be quite disciplined, but I'm not perfect. It was hard to choose to set aside time for this long-term project when I would rather do short-term wins. Also, having to follow a fairly strict formula instead of my more natural style

of writing made writing more difficult. Finally, I was scared. I was afraid that I would put all this work into my proposal and no publisher would accept it, and it would be a huge waste of time, and I would feel like a failure. Because I knew I would experience strong emotional resistance to making time for this activity, I set up a plan and accountability systems to keep me on track.

The book I used to help guide my process was entitled, *Nonfiction Book Proposals Anybody Can Write*, by Elizabeth Lyon. (There are many other good guides out there, but I chose this one because a friend who had gotten a contract with Random House recommended it.) To start, I set out a schedule of reading a portion of the book each week and working on one of the sections of my book proposal. Additionally, I had my assistant help me with different things, such as doing market research and formatting different sections of the proposal. Also, I committed to telling my assistant, my accountability partner, and my dad what I did on the book each week. Even with all this structure in place, I still had some starts and stops and times of lesser and greater productivity. In the end, though, I could push through this resistance and get the book proposal done, even though I often didn't feel like working on it.

> **TIME COACHING TIP**
>
> Before success comes a whole lot of risk of things not going right and a whole lot of negative feelings. But whether you succeed or not has much to do with whether you're willing to persevere despite this resistance.

Getting Feedback

I'm a super sweet, positive Midwesterner, so the idea of getting feedback, especially from the not-so-delicate world of New York publishing, was intimidating. But I knew that I needed to show my proposal not only to friends and family but also to book experts who could give me perspective on where I stood. And they told me. Sometimes in not very soft terms. Ouch. In one written vent session, I typed out in frustration:

I hate this.
This is annoying.

I don't like negative feedback.

I don't like discouragement.

I don't like rejection.

This is taking too long.

But . . . I didn't stop. I kept at it—writing, rewriting, and rewriting once more and continuing to get feedback. With the amazing encouragement of key professional advocates such as Cal Newport, a fantastic writer and productivity expert who wrote this book's foreword, and personal supporters such as my awesome parents and friends, I continued on.

Year Two

So I started and completed my book proposal in 2011. Now, in 2012, the goal was to find a book agent. Through a series of fortunate events, I got connected with someone who liked his book agent and offered to do an introduction. The meeting was successful. Voilà! In just a matter of weeks, I had a book agent who believed in me and my ideas, and the feeling of having a true team member infused me with energy.

My agent and I went back and forth for a few weeks, making some minor edits to my proposal. We set up a system where we would have a call for him to give me my assignments, I would make the changes, and then we would discuss any further changes on our next call.

Once the proposal was ready, we sent it off . . . and waited. This was the most nerve-wracking time of the entire process for me. I tried not to think about it too much because at this point there was nothing more I could do. My book proposal, my idea, my concept was on the auction block. And if no publisher accepted it, I would have to bury it in the never-accepted-book-proposal cemetery and start over, unless I wanted to self-publish. So I waited . . . and I did shed some tears when I found out about what my agent kindly called publishers "passing" but which really meant that my proposal was rejected. Sad.

One Magical Week

But then—literally within the span of a week—everything changed. It was Monday, April 30, 2012, and I opened my inbox to see an e-mail from my agent saying that an editor from McGraw-Hill was interested in my pro-

posal. I also read an e-mail on the same morning that said my first article for the *Harvard Business Review*, "The Thought-Patterns of Success," was going live.

Wow! Energy and excitement surged in me, and hope erupted as I thought this really might just happen. The impossible may come true.

And it did. I got an offer from McGraw-Hill, which led to this book. It takes a cheering squad to win a book contract. I never would have made it without the systems that I put in place for receiving incredible support and accountability from my family, friends, business contacts, book agent, and book editor.

Why Be Accountable?

Even as someone who specializes in helping people invest time in their highest priorities and who actively lives out what she teaches, I need support. Through my work and life, I've observed that the highest achievers don't deny their weaknesses; they acknowledge them and find out what systems and people they need to put in place to stay on track.

Marshall Goldsmith, author of *What Got You Here Won't Get You There*,[1] agrees. In his chapter entitled, "Following Up: You Do Not Get Better Without Follow-up," he shares this insight based on data analysis of over 86,000 people who went through leadership development training:

> *Real leadership development involves a process that takes time. . . . The process is a lot like physical exercise. Imagine having out-of-shape people sit in a room and listen to a speech on the importance of exercising, then watch some tapes on how to exercise, and perhaps then spend a few minutes simulating the act of exercising. Would you be surprised if all the people in the room were still unfit a year later? The source of physical fitness is not understanding the theory of working out. It is engaging in regular exercise.*
>
> *Well that pretty much sums up the value of executive development* **without follow-up**. *Nobody ever changed for the better by going to a training session. They got better by doing what they learned in the program.*

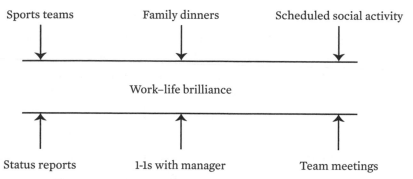

FIGURE 8.1 *Accountability to support work-life brilliance.*

This study included data from executive development training, but whether you find yourself at the top or the bottom of the organizational chart, accountability matters. With so many pressures trying to push you to invest your time in lower priorities, accountability can help you to stay aligned with your personal definition of success. It also helps you to balance and rebalance in response to the dynamic nature of life we discussed in Chapter 4. In the following pages you'll discover how to develop the proper accountability structures to keep you on track and to help you achieve work-life brilliance (Figure 8.1).

TABLE 8.1 *Key Mental Shift: Accountability*

HARMFUL	HELPFUL
I should be able to make myself do the right thing, so needing accountability means that I'm lazy, insecure, and inadequate.	If I find something difficult to do on my own, I will achieve better results if I put the right accountability structures in place.

Honesty: Be Accountable to Yourself

Before you ask for any outside support, you need to get extremely honest with yourself about these three points:

- **What do I really want?** If you haven't already documented your personal definition of success, you can find exercises in Chapter 4 to help

you write one. Also, decide what routines you actually need to follow to keep yourself aligned with your personal definition of success. I have a huge amount of respect for David Allen's *Getting Things Done* system, but for many people, it's too complex. If you just want to keep an up-to-date to-do list and regularly check your calendar so that you don't forget major responsibilities, admit it. This authenticity about your macro- and micro-level goals must come first so that you don't end up resisting the process, resenting the people keeping you accountable, and not creating a lasting behavioral change.

- **What can I really do?** As we discussed in Chapter 5, realistic expectations of yourself and others play an essential role in feeling good about what you do and don't do. Before you ask someone to hold you accountable, assess whether your desired actions will lead to a sustainable schedule given your current reality. Also decide how you will adjust your expectations for special circumstances, such as being sick, traveling out of town, or having extra meetings.
- **How will I track results?** Developing a routine for regular tracking and assessment of your key actions will give you clarity on what you've actually done. This will allow you to engage in meaningful accountability and keep you from these two extremes: being overly self-critical and discounting what you did well or being overly self-indulgent and giving yourself too many allowances to deviate from your routines. This could look as basic as making a hash mark on a paper for each time you call a new prospective client or as sophisticated as running detailed reports in a project management system.

These two simple examples illustrate what honest self-accountability can look like professionally and personally.

Keeping on Top of Industry News

- **What I really want.** I want to keep on top of current reports, news, or papers in my field without getting distracted and not doing my work.
- **What I can really do.** I can spend 30 minutes a day when I'm sitting on the train reading industry updates.
- **How I will track results.** For every day that I read industry news on the train but not outside that time, I will give myself a point on an Excel

sheet. When I accumulate 20 points, I will reward myself by buying a new book and spending a whole day reading.

Losing Weight

- **What I really want.** I want to consistently lose weight.
- **What I can really do.** I don't have more time to exercise, so instead I will cut my calorie intake.
- **How I will track results.** On a daily basis, I will put my food intake into a calorie counter and stop eating when I reach my daily maximum. On a weekly basis, I will weigh myself and keep a record of my numbers. I will use my weight numbers as feedback on how I need to adjust my eating in the coming week. I will celebrate—in a non-food-related way—when I hit certain goals.

Once you've gotten honest with yourself, you may have the ability to keep up your routines on your own. If so, fantastic! You don't need to put in any more levels of accountability. However, if you find that self-tracking isn't enough to maintain your motivation, you need to enlist outside support.

SCARED OF THE NUMBERS?

If the idea of measuring your actions terrifies you because you have a propensity toward feeling easily discouraged and defeated, check out the "Zooming in to Avoid Overwhelm" routine in the "Quick Reference Done-for-You Routines and Tools" section at the end of Chapter 7. This exercise allows you to evaluate your progress without beating yourself up.

Transparency: Be Accountable to a Person

How you invested your time as a child probably had much to do with accountability to key individuals in your life. Your mom woke you up in the morning. Your older brother yelled at you if you didn't leave for the bus on time. Your teacher asked you for homework and graded your exams. Your best friend practiced soccer with you after school. Your dad turned off the TV and sent you to bed.

Then you became a "grown-up," and suddenly you had responsibility to go through your day without all these prompts. If you have a strong internal sense of order, this transition probably happened seamlessly; if you don't, it might have been disastrous. Either way, we all have areas of our life where self-accountability doesn't provide enough force to keep us aligned with our highest priorities. In those instances, we need to put in accountability to another person.

Here's a guide to creating greater transparency in the areas where you consistently don't do what you want to do:

- **Who to ask.** The person who keeps you accountable plays a major role in the success of this strategy. Look for someone you can count on to pick up the phone or to respond to your e-mail or simply to talk to you when you see each other. It's demotivating when you feel like a person doesn't care. Also look for someone who will put courage, defined by Merriam-Webster as the "mental or moral strength to venture, persevere, and withstand danger, fear, or difficulty," into you through encouragement. You can ask a friend, a significant other, a coworker, or a family member to support you. But if you can't practice total transparency with these individuals, it may make sense to enlist an outside coach, trainer, tutor, or mentor to help. It's easier for someone to remain impartial and calm when your choices don't have a direct impact on their lives. A professional accountability partner will rarely blurt out, "I can't believe you spent *that* much last week!"

- **When to connect.** Your frequency of contact depends on how much support you need to bring about the desired change. Typically, daily or weekly check-ins work best. But you can find your correct level of accountability through experimentation. For instance, maybe you find that you forget to make your new routine a priority if you only have a weekly call, so then you decide to have more frequent calls or to check in by text or e-mail on a daily basis. On the other hand, once you've strengthened your routines, you may find that you only need to connect with an accountability partner once a month. Tighten or loosen the reins as needed to gain the desired results.

- **What to discuss.** Accountability can encompass everything from how much water you drank to how nice you were to your coworkers to

whether you invested time in an important project. You can narrow or broaden the scope as desired. But you should only ask for accountability on activities you want to change right now so that you don't feel unnecessarily guilty for not doing items that you don't see as a current priority. You also want to make sure that you talk to the right person about the right topics. You could very well have a personal trainer who listens to you divulge how many push-ups you did last week and a university colleague that acts as a sounding board for your research on food bacteria.

- **How to proceed.** Once you've asked the person if he or she has the willingness and ability to help keep you accountable, you can come up with a structure for your interactions. As a conversation, it may look as formal as a set series of questions that the person asks and you answer with a "Yes" or "No" or as loose as a 30- to 60-minute phone call where you wax poetic on your current project status and the person gives you insight and feedback on how to proceed. As an e-mail or text, it could look like simply sending a note that says, "Wrote for an hour," or it could appear as an essay on your thoughts related to a manuscript. Once again, do what works. You want to have the right kind of transparency to conjure up the discipline to practice your routines consistently. And if it makes sense, you can engage in mutual accountability, where you not only receive accountability but also help the other person move forward on his or her goals.

Camaraderie: Be Accountable to a Group

Individual accountability has the advantage of custom fitting to your various needs. But group accountability provides some of the most powerful support for investing your time in what you want to do in a particular area of your life, even when you don't feel like it. By deciding in advance that you want to take a class, join a running club, participate in Weight Watchers, or go to a book club, you dramatically increase your probability of engaging in the related activity. By definition, these groups provide structure that forces you to allocate your time in a certain way through meetings, homework, and other commitments. Also, the positive peer pressure works wonders. Would you go out running on your own at 6 a.m.

KEEPING OTHERS ACCOUNTABLE
WITHOUT FEELING LIKE A MICROMANAGER

Sometimes as the leader, manager, or supervisor, you need to fill the role of keeping others accountable. If you tend to prefer a huge amount of autonomy in your work, the idea of telling people what to do by a certain time can seem really uncomfortable. But, keeping others accountable in the right way gives them the ability to succeed. Here are a few tips from Louis Lautman[2], founder of www.supremeoutsourc-ing.com, on how to help others invest their time effectively without feeling like a micromanager:

- Hire high-performance individuals who have a track record of high-quality work.
- From the beginning, let them know the reality of what you expect, and get agreement on the terms of the relationship. When you delegate work, seek agreement on the deliverables and how and when they will be delivered.
- If you are not working with high-performance individuals, insist on even greater clarity on agreements and measurements. Once they know what is expected of them, they should deliver on time or know that if they are not going to deliver on time, they should tell you in advance so that you can plan accordingly. It is all about setting and managing the proper expectations.
- If you see that you gave them too much freedom and didn't get what you want, this is where you not as a manager but as a leader need to inspire these people to deliver quality, timely results.

Do you see how the strategies Lautman suggested do not relate to pressuring people to perform? Instead, healthy accountability benefits everyone by clarifying the priorities, setting realistic expectations, and then engaging in routine follow-up. With this kind of management style, your focus is on everyone adhering to the mutual agreements, not you nagging others to get things done.

on a Saturday morning? Most likely not. But if you know that a whole crew of running buddies will have dragged themselves out of bed to get there, you'll find a way to show up.

These guidelines can help you find the right group accountability for support and camaraderie in reaching shared goals:

- **Be honest.** Before throwing yourself into a group, make sure that it aligns with what you discovered in the "Honesty: Be Accountable to Yourself" section. If you don't really care about what the other group members care about, you'll end up feeling like an imposter. Also, if you have different expectations, such as you want to meet other professionals in your industry once a month and the group requires attendance at weekly meetings, you'll end up frustrated. Clubs, classes, "masterminds," networking meetings, recovery groups, and religious organizations come in all different forms, so find one that feels right for you.

- **Be aware.** Group accountability has the benefit of bringing you together with other people for support and advice in how to overcome a challenge or do what you want to do in a particular area. But some of these groups can create an overly critical or judgmental environment with a skewed sense of required versus optional behavior. If you find that participation in a group makes you feel scared, sick, judged, afraid, overwhelmed, or unbalanced or leads to you neglecting other important priorities in your life, you may want to reconsider your membership. These groups should make you feel more supported, not more isolated.

- **Be open.** In-person groups have the greatest power to direct your time investment, but other types of communities can work too. You can search for writers groups, research groups, productivity groups, cooking groups, and all sorts of other clusters of people with similar interests online. With these, you will just need to decide to spend the right amount of time on a regular basis engaging in them. Another possibility is to have a group where you all connect via Skype or a conference call number such as those available at www.freeconferencecall.com. If you're a business professional who travels a great deal for work, this sort of virtual "mastermind" group could allow you to more consistently connect with others.

Often this group accountability will encompass specific goals or hobbies in your life. But if you can find or found a company culture that provides the right type of accountability to achieve your priorities, it can act as a powerful form of group accountability for professional achievement.

Culture: Accountability Routines at Work

The mention of accountability routines in the workplace makes many people nervous because it usually means items such as quotas and yearly reviews and standardized test scores. Although these accountability measures may have some effectiveness (I won't debate that topic here), they rarely encourage the most effective investment of time both personally and professionally. In my research for this book, I came across some businesses that provide excellent examples of accountability routines that work toward helping employees achieve more success with less stress. Counterintuitively, systems that actively encourage employees to stop working lead to higher productivity. If you're a business leader, take note.

Adobe: Real Vacation Time

In today's fast-paced, highly connected work culture, the start of your career usually signals the end of any real vacation. Even when people do technically have the ability to take time off, many don't or they check in during the time meant for an entire mental break from work. (One of my friends does an informal survey of current employees whenever she interviews for a new job to find out whether people actually use their vacation time.)

Adobe's vacation policies stand in stark contrast to the general trend toward thwarting employees' efforts to disengage from work. Not only does the company give a generous amount of time off, but also it has built routines into the company culture to make real vacations possible.

Adobe Systems senior vice president of human resources, Donna Morris,[3] offered some great insight to me on why the company actively works toward helping employees take vacation:

Why does Adobe offer a holiday shutdown in North American offices the week of July 4 and the week between Christmas and New Year's?

We've all felt the pain of coming back from vacation to an inbox full of e-mails, meetings, and tasks. The benefits of vacation quickly melt away as you work at a feverish pace to catch up. With Adobe's holiday shutdowns, our employees are off at the same time, so we can truly unwind. We work really hard to meet our project commitments ahead of shutdown. We've been able to effectively achieve our goals while at the same time offering this valuable benefit.

Adobe offers benefits like a four-week sabbatical after every five years of service. What do you see as the advantage of this break in routine?

As an IP-based company, Adobe's most valuable asset is its employees. Providing time-off programs like sabbaticals is really an investment in our people and by extension the company. Whether they spend time learning a new language, traveling the globe, or simply spending quality time with their family at home, employees come back from sabbatical with a renewed sense of commitment to the company and their role. They are re-energized, have a fresh perspective on challenges they need to solve, and offer creative ideas to make an impact.

In addition to these two fixed times off with paid holiday shutdowns and sabbaticals, Adobe offers employees time away from the office to balance work and life. "For example, in the United States, employees are not given a set number of days for vacation," Morris explains. "They simply work with their manager to take the time they need." By having these kinds of policies in place, Adobe not only gives employees time off but also actively encourages them to take it.

Boston Consulting Group: Time to Disconnect

Major blocks of time away play an important role in your health and well-being, but they're not enough. On a daily and weekly basis, your mind and body need the opportunity to reset, recharge, prepare, and sim-

ply get things done. High-intensity work environments, such as Boston Consulting Group, tend toward creating a company culture that works against balance. When Leslie Perlow,[4] Konosuke Matsushita Professor of Leadership at Harvard Business School, first did a survey of 1,600 of the firm's managers and professionals, 92 percent of them worked over 50 hours a week, and one-third of them logged 65 or more hours a week. Additionally, everyone constantly monitored their smartphones for any sign of new information. This constant connection created a vicious cycle of instant responsiveness that made putting in as many hours as possible an expected part of the company culture. Individuals couldn't escape this spiral alone—it required a team effort.

Perlow began experimenting with a team approach to spending time disconnected from technology. Despite initial resistance and skepticism to the idea by some individuals, the numbers proved this predictable time off (PTO) approach works. Teams using the PTO approach rated this way versus teams not using it:

- 23 percent higher in job satisfaction
- 16 percent more satisfied with work-life balance
- 23 percent increase in rating their team as doing everything it could to be efficient
- 23 percent increase in rating their team as doing everything it could to be effective

Four years after the first experiment, 86 percent of the consulting staff in the firm's Northeast offices engage in this simple but powerful PTO approach that Perlow explains more deeply in *Sleeping with Your Smartphone: How to Break the 24/7 Habit and Change the Way You Work.* Here's an introduction to the basics of this method[5]:

- **Shared weekly PTO goal.** The team agrees on a unit of predictable time off that everyone will personally work to achieve and help others to accomplish. Potential PTO goals could include times disconnected from wireless devices, e-mail blackouts where no one reads or answers e-mails, and uninterrupted blocks of work time.

- **Weekly PTO discussions.** Each week, team members gather to talk about how they did personally on the PTO goal. Individuals also share how they feel in general about their work and lives and the sustainability of their current way of working given their personal circumstances. The point of this review is to empower each person and the team as a whole to work together in achieving the coming week's goal.
- **Team leader support.** The team leader needs to have openness to experimenting with this method instead of resisting it. The PTO method requires a shared process of discovery and collaboration on how to support one another and be more efficient and effective as a team.

Through this process, Boston Consulting Group is actively working into their company culture accountability routines that enable employees to unplug for at least one block of time each week. But . . . some companies have taken this idea even further. You're about to witness what it can look like for an *entire* company to have built into every part of its culture the three secrets that I've shared in this book.

Menlo Innovations: This Works Better for the Humans

Menlo's mission is to "end human suffering as it relates to technology." But that means not only producing software that works wonders for the end user, which the company does brilliantly, but also creating an entire company culture around working at a humanly sustainable pace. I had the privilege of visiting the company's offices, which it dubs the Menlo Software Factory. Within that space, I witnessed how many of the principles I advocate for on an individual level could play out in a 40-person company that prides itself on employees working only 40 hours a week and completely disconnecting during vacation.

Here's what I discovered on a tour led by Rich Sheridan, president, CEO, and chief storyteller at Menlo:

- **Client selection.** Menlo only works with clients who respect its approach to work. The company has fired highly profitable clients and let go of sales staff because they prioritized making deals over

finding a cultural fit. Despite this unwavering commitment to its ideals—or maybe because of it—the company made the list of *Inc.* magazine's "500 Fastest Growing Companies" in 2006 and its list of "5,000 Fastest Growing Private Companies in America" in 2007, 2008, 2009, and 2012.

- **Employee integration.** At Menlo, all work happens in pairs. Two people share a computer and together complete one activity at a time. This leads to quick problem solving because you never get stuck on a problem alone. It also means that during the day, you completely focus on work because someone not only is watching you but also is literally working with you all the time. Because of the completely collaborative nature of the company, the interview process includes multiple days of working within the business to see if you play well with others.

- **Weekly switch-up.** Except for project managers, everyone else switches pairs on a weekly basis. It is also possible for an individual to switch projects on this weekly boundary. This is a routine way that Menlo keeps variety in the work when projects literally can stretch out for longer than seven years.

- **Ambiguity elimination.** The constant shuffle of pairs and projects requires total clarity on project status and upcoming steps. These planning routines keep everyone on track:
  - **Weekly kickoff.** At this meeting, the team goes through the current project status.
  - **Daily standup.** Each morning, the entire company stands in a circle, and each pair briefly explains what they're working on now. According to Sheridan, it never takes longer than 13 minutes to make it around the 40-person ring.
  - **Weekly show and tell.** At the end of each week, the clients come into the office to view the current progress. Based on the results of the last week, the clients decide which priorities they want to have in place for the coming week using weekly planning sheets.
  - **Weekly planning sheets.** Each of these sheets of paper contains a large rectangle representing the 40-hour workweek for a two-person project team. The template already has eight hours blocked off for repetitive and predictable elements of Menlo's

process, including time for estimation, show and tell, kickoff, daily standup, and casual project communication time. The clients fill in the remaining 32 hours with story cards, which each represent a particular remaining task to complete on the project. Each story card includes a time estimate and is folded in proportion to the number of hours it will take to complete. For instance, a four-hour task is twice as tall as a two-hour task. This allows clients to make choices about action-based priorities and to set realistic time and budget expectations because it's completely obvious if something doesn't fit (Figure 8.2).

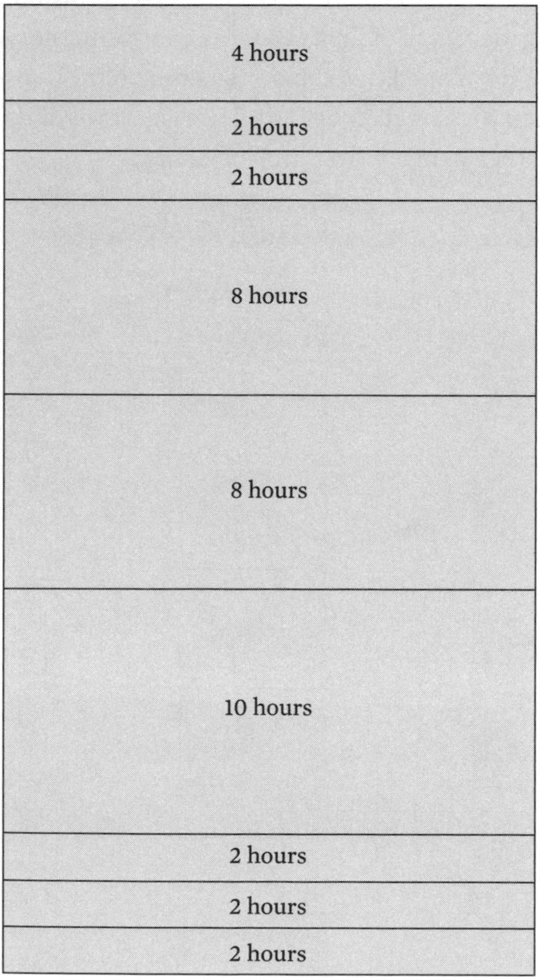

FIGURE 8.2 *Menlo weekly planning sheets.*

- **Weekly project board.** The project manager then unfolds the story cards placed on the weekly planning sheets and posts them in a grid on the wall. The columns represent each pair for the week and the rows each day from Monday through Friday. Menlo has found that this simple, visual, public system of planning and accountability works far better for the company than more sophisticated project management software. With a quick glance, anyone can see what the teams have done, what they're doing now, and what's next (Figure 8.3).

- **Fear removal.** Menlo strives to eliminate fear as a motivator. In a practical sense, this means that you never face punishment for underestimating the length of time needed to complete a story card. Instead, Menlo has developed this standard method of response:

  - As soon as team members realize that they will go over the estimate, they contact their project manager.

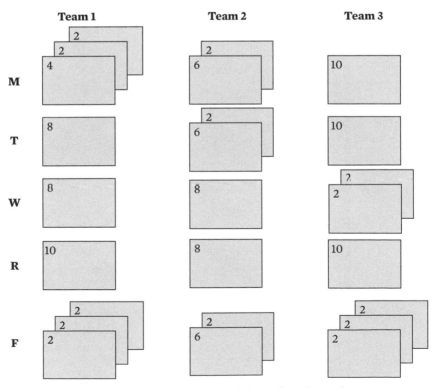

FIGURE 8.3 *Menlo weekly project board.*

- Their project manager thanks them for delivering the information. (They're trained not to cringe!)
- Everyone talks about it.
- If the situation can't be resolved internally, the company calls the clients to discuss what they would like to do in light of the increased time and budget requirements. The clients decide whether the team should still take the action, stop, or move on to another step.
- No one is pressured to stay late or to come in on the weekend to just "get it done."

- **Work-life separation.** The software factory has some super family-friendly policies such as allowing infants to come with their parents to work for six to nine months. In general, though, work-life separation rules. No one has a work laptop, and internal communication happens face-to-face, so it's not necessary or possible to bring work home. No one works alone, and everyone has accountability to complete his or her assigned activities, leaving no room for personal calls, texts, social media, or e-mail during work hours.

Menlo's culture demonstrates a number of important principles, such as the importance of planning routines and how realistic expectations force solid decisions about priorities. But I most appreciate that this entire system focuses on what works best for people to invest their time well and produce the most value for clients instead of sacrificing peoples' health and sanity for the sake of production goals detached from reality. Menlo's culture also extends into their client relationships. Menlo regularly trades a significant portion of its cash revenue for stock in its clients' companies and future royalties in the products it helps its clients bring to market. In this way, the company is clearly stating how much it believes in the results of this sustainable human pace.

· ·
Journaling Exercise: Structural Support

From the beginning, I've emphasized that you need to exercise your ability to make a choice about how you invest your time. But that doesn't mean you have to do everything on your own.

The key to success in lasting behavior change is building the right structural support into your life. Answer these journaling questions to give you direction on how to make this happen.

Journaling Questions

- Have I gotten honest with myself, including clarifying what I really want, what I can really do, and how I will track my results?

- Would I like one-on-one accountability? If so, is there already a person in my life who can play this role, or do I need to seek someone out?

- Do I want to join a group? If so, which one, and how much can I realistically participate in it?

Acknowledging that you need help plays a huge role in your success. If you think you might need support in implementing these principles from Real Life E Time Coaching and Training, visit www.reallifee.com to find out more.

Coaching with Elizabeth has had a great impact on my life. I've worked on trying to improve my time management and organization for years, but going through a coaching series with her helped me actually get more of what I "know" into practice. It's not so much about what you should do (if it were, no one would struggle with weight loss, because all you need to do is "eat right and exercise"); it's about actually getting it into practice.

—INTERNAL IT BUSINESS CONSULTANT,
FORTUNE 100 COMPANY

Notes

1. Marshall Goldsmith and Mark Reiter, *What Got You Here Won't Get You There: How Successful People Become Even More Successful*. New York: Hyperion, 2007.

2. Louis Lautman, Founder, Supreme Outsourcing. Interview by Elizabeth Saunders, e-mail, July 2, 2012.

3. Donna Morris, Senior Vice President of Human Resources, Adobe Systems. Interview by Elizabeth Saunders, e-mail, July 11, 2012.

4. Leslie A. Perlow, "Breaking the Smartphone Addiction," HBS Working Knowledge. Available at: http://hbswk.hbs.edu/item/6877.html.

5. Leslie Perlow, "Predictable Time Off: The Team Solution to Overcoming Constant Work Connection," *Fast Company*. Available at: www.fastcompany .com/1837867/predictable-time-off-the-team-solution-to-overcoming-constant -workplace-connection.

CHAPTER 9

TIME PEACE

Reduce Time-Caused Drama

War is easy. Peace is the difficult prize.

—SIR HUGH ORDE, FORMER CHIEF CONSTABLE
OF THE POLICE SERVICE OF NORTHERN IRELAND

The Burned Casserole

Thunk. Lucy's mobile phone smacked against the side of her handbag before landing on a paper-clipped pile of receipts ordered by purchase date. "I can't believe that he did this again!" Lucy exclaimed at her cat, who let out a sympathetic meow on cue.

Jason, Lucy's boyfriend, had forgotten about their plans to meet friends for dinner at 7 p.m. until 6:45 p.m. He had just called to apologize and to let Lucy know he was walking out of the office.

Lucy fidgeted about the house, straightening pillows, applying lipstick, drying dishes, looking at the microwave clock, checking on her casserole, and doing anything else she could think of to keep herself occupied. She was so looking forward to this dinner party and to showing off her culinary prowess. Over the weekend, she had bought special ingredients, and today she skipped her lunch break so that she could get home in time to bake a casserole from her grandmother's recipe.

With each passing minute, she got more and more agitated, and her thoughts became more and more negative: "How could Jason just forget we had plans with friends? Does he even care? Doesn't he know that our

friends have kids who need to go to bed early? Why can't he just get his act together?"

Jason meanwhile trotted briskly to the train station and congratulated himself on bounding down the steps fast enough to catch the next train. He phoned a few friends during his ride home, picked up his car, drove the most efficient route, and burst in the door at about 7:20 p.m. rather pleased at his near-record time.

Far from impressed, Lucy turned toward him with a scowl. "I already told Patty and George we'll arrive late," she snapped. "I'll get the casserole out of the oven. You grab a pinot noir from the wine rack."

"I wonder what's bothering her?" Jason thought, as he went to pick out a red with a slight oak.

An exclamation from the kitchen cut through the silent tension between them. "Oh nooooo!!!!"

"What's wrong?" Jason asked.

"My casserole is burned!" Lucy shouted, "And it's all your fault!"

"Can you scrape off the top?" Jason suggested as he moved toward the smoky haze in the kitchen.

"I don't think so," Lucy said with a whimper. "The crispy onion topping is one of the essential textures."

"Well maybe we can salvage some parts," Jason said and began to scoop the charred bits into a dish and get the casserole to a point where it looked somewhat edible.

Lucy and Jason headed out the door. Jason once again quite pleased with his casserole salvaging skills, and Lucy totally mortified that her careful preparation had led to naught: Her casserole had burned, and they would arrive an hour late for dinner.

So goes a time personality conflict. . . . Most people don't wake up in the morning thinking: I really want to frustrate everyone around me. But when time personalities clash, either at home or at work, your actions can be perceived as inconsiderate, annoying, or even downright disrespectful. And you can end up feeling resentful, guilty, and totally frustrated.

But there is a better way. Through my work as a time coach and personal life experience, I've seen that you can reduce time-caused drama

with the proper understanding of one another's perspectives and the right tools for adapting, communicating, and recovering.

What Frustrates Planners About Spontaneous People and Vice Versa

If you've ever struggled in relationships with people with a different time personality than yourself and wondered, "What could they possibly be thinking?" you're in luck. Right now, you're about to get some insight into what's going on inside their minds. The following explanations will help you to better understand both perspectives, whether you struggle with conflicts with your significant other, a colleague, a boss, a child, a client, or a friend.

The Planner Perspective

- **What makes them feel bad about themselves?** When they can't get everything done on their list. When life doesn't go according to their plans. When they're surprised. When things take longer than expected. When they didn't anticipate and proactively address a potential problem.
- **Why?** Their plan is their personal "measuring stick" of the success of their day. They like looking forward to things, knowing that they can get everything done, and feeling in control. Closing off possibilities and finishing things feels good to them.
- **What can frustrate them about spontaneous people?** When they can't make plans because they haven't received a definite commitment. When they were looking forward to something and then it doesn't happen. When they take time and thought to prepare something only to have the preparations come to nothing when the plans change. When they must do a great deal of things last minute and at a frenzied pace because of others' lack of planning.
- **Why?** Because having a plan makes planners feel secure, not being able to make one puts them on edge. They can't know for certain whether or not they can commit to activities. They can't anticipate

and prepare for events. Also, they tend to see making plans to do something or spend time with someone as a sign of valuing that activity or relationship. This means that they can feel unvalued and unappreciated when people won't make or keep plans with them, such as the example with Lucy at the start of the chapter.

The Spontaneous Perspective

- **What makes them feel bad about themselves?** When they let people down. When they forget things. When they constantly feel in crisis mode (even though they thrive on working in bursts of energy). When they don't return messages or make plans with friends. When they can't trust themselves to be able to start on something when they want to do so or to get it done on time. When they are late. When they have lots of unfinished projects in their life.
- **Why?** In general, people who are spontaneous want to be responsive and open to what is happening around them and want to make people happy; they just can't necessarily plan on what will happen. They often don't feel in control of or don't want to control their external circumstances. Because of this more fluid, in-the-moment approach to the outside world, they don't want to make too many commitments for fear of the expectations that will be placed on them that they may or may not be able to meet.
- **What frustrates them about planners?** When they are asked to make commitments days or weeks in advance when they would really just prefer to wake up and see what they feel like doing. When they are asked to stick with the plan because it was the plan not because it is still the best option. When they know things won't always go according to plan, so they feel like planning is a waste of time and not based in reality.
- **Why?** Because new ideas and possibilities and surprises thrill them, making plans before they know every possible option and exactly how they will feel at the moment seems horribly restrictive. They don't want to commit to something and then miss out on something better. They can't stand the idea of forcing themselves to do something they don't feel like doing at the time. This means any sort of plan can seem

like an ominous weight. Instead of being seen as an honor to have plans made with them, it can instead feel controlling.

Did you recognize yourself in either of these categories? Most people tend to fall into one or the other category, but some people flip between the two in different situations, such as work versus home. If you have been experiencing any of the frustrations just listed, I would like you to reread the opposite perspective. That will help you to understand and maybe even appreciate the other side. This expanded insight into the opposite perspective will help you to let go of negative interpretations of people's motives, which can lead to unhealthy criticism and contempt. Once you have put yourself in a more positive mind-set toward the person, you have a much greater ability to work on improving the situation.

Example:

- **Lucy could think:** Jason didn't mean to disappoint or frustrate me. He simply got tied up in a meeting and lost track of the time. I appreciate his efforts to get home so quickly.
- **Jason could think:** I know Lucy puts a great deal of forethought into cooking, and it's important to her to arrive on time to events. To show that I value her feelings, I need to find better ways to remember after-work appointments.

TABLE 9.1 *Key Mental Shift: Time Personality*

HARMFUL	HELPFUL
This person is purposely trying to annoy and frustrate me and to disregard my needs.	This person has a different approach toward time investment than I do, so I need to work on communicating my needs and expectations and understanding the opposite perspective.

What You Can Do (Even If the Other Person Doesn't Change)

Although it's tempting to think that life would be perfect if everyone else would just change, this attitude actually can leave you feeling helpless and disempowered. Other people may or may not decide to adapt their style,

but you do have the power to modify your own thoughts, emotions, and actions. This is why the second stage of time peace examines what you can change about yourself before attempting to address issues with other people. This is a good strategy not only from the standpoint that you are focusing on the areas within your control but also from the standpoint that other people in your life will tend to be more open to change when they see how hard you're trying.

Asking yourself how you can think or act differently to lessen conflict at home, at work, or in other areas of your life takes a great deal of humility and maturity. It forces you to practice Stephen Covey's principle of "begin with the end in mind" from *The 7 Habits of Highly Effective People.*[1] Instead of focusing on being right, having what you prefer, or winning, you're focusing on building the relationship, reducing conflict, and accomplishing the end goal, whether it's completing a presentation or having a clean house. These sorts of incremental changes can have a big impact.

Empowerment for the Spontaneous

- **When you're tempted to be annoyed at planners.** Review the "Planner Perspective," discussed in the last section, and remind yourself that they're not trying to be controlling or frustrating. Separate how their actions make you initially feel from their actual motives.
- **Give yourself freedom to be spontaneous in certain areas.** If you're naturally spontaneous, always having structure will drive you crazy. Decide on which parts of your life require a higher level of planning discipline, and give yourself freedom to go with the flow in the rest.
- **If almost all your life needs to be planned.** Permit yourself to have some sort of choice within designated blocks of time, such as the freedom to spontaneously decide where you work or what you order for lunch or which e-mail you answer first.
- **If you really resist planning a certain activity.** Ask yourself whether or not you really need to do the activity in the first place. If you determine that you do really want or need to do it, figure out what exactly is bothering you about planning it into your schedule: Is it the time of day? The people involved? Some other emotional or mental resistance?

- **If you have a tendency to forget your commitments.** It's time for you to figure out a consistent calendar, to-do list, or other method that you can use to record what you said you would do, to remind you of commitments, and to check before agreeing to new items.
- **If you have a tendency to overestimate how much can fit in a day.** Begin to review your actual versus intended level of activity each day. This will give you clarity on what's possible and allow you to set realistic expectations. This practice will help you to get comfortable embracing the reality of 24 hours in a day and seven days in a week instead of denying it. (You'll be much happier—guaranteed.)
- **If you won't make personal commitments because work feels overwhelming.** Think very carefully about what you really want out of life and what sacrifices you are willing to make to get there. Although working long hours is necessary sometimes, making this a lifestyle can jeopardize your relationships and sense of self outside work. Plus, longer hours don't necessarily lead to higher productivity because typically your motivation, focus, and energy decrease when you put in many extra hours.

OPEN COMMUNICATION POLICY

One of the ways to make planners most upset is to deviate from a plan and not let them know what's happening. If you need to change something at the last minute, tell them, apologize if appropriate, and make it clear what's happening now. This will increase planners' sense of security and reduce the danger of them assuming negative motives.

Empowerment for the Planners

- **When you're tempted to be annoyed at spontaneous people.** Review the "Spontaneous Perspective" described previously, and remind yourself that they're not trying to make you feel insecure or unvalued. Also remember that they most likely never thought of making plans, not that they thought of making them and just didn't follow through in order to spite you.

- **Make plans to make plans.** If a spontaneous person isn't ready to commit to an activity, ask him or her if you can follow up at a certain time (i.e., making a plan to make a plan) or simply make a note to yourself to follow up on a specific date. This gives you security that you have at least nailed down a follow-up.

- **If you really need to decide something for yourself.** Book a ticket, commit to a project, RSVP for an event, or do whatever else you need to do to make sure that you can make the plans that matter to you. This may mean that your spontaneous friend or coworker may or may not be part of what you do. But you've empowered yourself to not miss out because someone else won't commit.

- **Decide what's really important to plan.** Although you may prefer to keep everything on schedule all the time (horror of horrors when you have to interrupt your rituals for an unexpected disturbance), not everything *has* to be planned. By getting clear on what's really important and what can be flexible, you put less pressure on yourself and on the spontaneous people in your life. For instance, maybe you decide on a day to meet up with someone but don't choose the exact time and location until the morning of the meet up.

- **Keep things tentative.** Spontaneous people often have more openness to plans if you make them "tentative" and then offer to confirm a few days in advance. This makes them feel like they have a way out and relieves some of the pressure.

- **If you get really upset when plans change.** Challenge yourself to think through exactly what made you disappointed or angry. Was it a matter of feeling in control or secure? Did you feel disrespected or unappreciated? Figure out exactly what thoughts and emotions the event triggered, and then decide whether or not they are a reflection of something that needs to change in someone else or a reflection of what you need to adjust inside yourself.

- **If you shut down when the unexpected happens.** Stop and say to yourself, "My day hasn't gone as I expected. But what can I do to make the best of the current situation?" Focus on what you can control and your current options instead of obsessing about what can't happen and doing nothing.

I hope that these tips give you a good start at creating more time peace in your life. You have far more power than you may have previously realized to improve your experience of the situation without anyone else changing at all. But, if even after understanding the opposite perspective and adjusting your methods you still feel frustrated, it may be time to talk through the situation with the other person involved in the conflict.

How to Communicate About Your Needs Instead of Retreating or Exploding

We'll soon take a look at how to approach talking to someone with the opposite time personality in a constructive manner. But before we do, I want you to ask yourself this final set of questions:

- **Is this conflict regarding something where there is an actual right or wrong answer and/or consequences for doing something in a certain way or is this simply a matter of preference?** (If it's simply a matter of preference, you may want to hold your tongue.)
- **Is there an unusual circumstance in my life or in the life of the other person that is increasing the intensity of our differences and/or my response to those differences?** (If there's a stressful situation such as an illness, a heavy travel schedule, or a major deadline, you may want to wait to see if things change after the season passes.)
- **Is this a pattern of behavior or an isolated incident?** (If this is highly unusual behavior, you may want to forgive and move on.)
- **Is this about something else?** That is, I want more help around the house but instead of saying that, I'm giving my significant other the silent treatment when he arrives home late? (If this is about something else other than time personalities, address the real issue instead of the surface one.)

Now we'll head into our feature presentation about talking through time personality conflicts. To increase your chance of a successful outcome, remember that timing is critical. If you already have a regular meeting designated for discussing any issues with your boss, significant other, coworker, etc., then try to confine this conversation to those times. But if

you don't have any kind of recurring check-in time, then use these guidelines to pick the best opportunity to bring up your concern:

- **Avoid transition times when people are just arriving or just leaving.** They tend to already feel in a rush and may feel stressed if they're running late.
- **Try not to talk to them when they're tired, hungry, drained, or angry.** They will have a lower capacity to respond well in those situations.
- **If they like warning before serious conversations, make a plan to talk with them instead of launching into the conversation without advance notice.**
- **Address situations that pass all the preceding cross-checks as soon as possible.** Increased time thinking through your problem over and over can lead to a buildup of more and more negative emotion.

Once you've picked a time, you can rehearse your strategy for having a discussion about the time conflict. If you're spontaneous, you may not like the idea of planning out your approach. But the point behind this is not to turn the conversation into a monologue or to be manipulative, but simply to override the more natural emotional response so that you can have a productive discussion. I've drawn this conversation outline from the book *Crucial Conversations: Tools for Talking When Stakes Are High*,[2] and I recommend that you check this book out if you would like further detail.

- **Share your facts.** Tell the other person what you observed, such as, "On Thursday, you arrived an hour later than you said you would for our meeting" or "I told you that I just wanted to relax at home over the weekend, and you still asked me every night this week where I wanted to go out on Saturday." Be especially careful to avoid harshness in your speech and criticism of someone's overall character.
- **Tell your story.** Now it's time to share how you interpreted those facts, such as, "When you showed up late, it made me afraid that you had forgotten about the meeting, and it made me feel angry that you didn't seem to value my time," or "When you kept asking where I wanted to go, it made me feel like you didn't respect my need to rest and that you were trying to convince me to do what you wanted."

- **Ask for others' paths.** Invite the other person to share his or her facts and stories by saying something like, "Can you explain to me your perspective on what happened on Thursday?" or "Can you help me to understand why you kept asking about Saturday?"
- **Talk tentatively.** This means that when you share your facts and tell your story, you keep the two separate. You don't state your story in such a way that it comes across as the only correct interpretation of the facts.
- **Encourage testing.** When you ask for others' paths, you want to do so in such a way that shows you're open to what they have to say, no matter how controversial. Be especially careful with your tone of voice, and give the other person ample time to respond.

This model can help you to come through a discussion in a productive manner instead of retreating or exploding. Practicing this technique on a consistent basis can also allow you to communicate clearly about your needs and wants without automatically eliciting defensiveness in other people. Even with the best of strategies, though, people of different time personalities will still upset you sometimes. So what do you do then?

How to Recover Quickly When You End Up Disappointed, Frustrated, or Angry

After an upset, you can follow these four steps to effectively process the situation and move on:

- **Step 1: Validate your feelings.** Even if the other person didn't mean to cause you harm, you have a right to feel how you feel. If you're hurt, upset, disappointed, frustrated, sad, or feeling any other emotion, that's okay. Own it and validate it instead of stuffing the fact that something said or not said, done or not done bothered you.
- **Step 2: Forgive the person.** *Forgiveness* literally means "to hurl away," "to release," or "to make oneself free," whereas *resentment* means to "feel again." Breaking free of reliving past hurt over and over again requires forgiveness.

- **If they've apologized.** Say, "I accept the apology, and I forgive you." Don't diminish your feelings and say, "No worries. It wasn't a big deal," if it was a big deal to you. Also, don't withhold forgiveness. Unforgiveness will not give you power but will instead trap you in a vicious cycle of control and revenge.

- **If they haven't apologized.** You may want to have a productive discussion, as described earlier. Or you simply may forgive people on your own—for your sake, not their sake. This could look like writing a letter (that you don't send to them) or when you have some time alone simply saying out loud: "[Name], I forgive you for [action or inaction], which made me feel [emotion]."

- **Step 3: Set boundaries.** Forgiving a person doesn't mean that you give that person license to perpetually hurt you. Here are a few ideas of how planners and spontaneous people can set boundaries personally and professionally:

  - **Planners' personal side.** Stop initiating one-on-one plans with people who constantly cancel and really hurt your feelings. Instead, invite them to group events where their presence is welcome but not essential, or wait for them to take the lead in setting something up.

  - **Planners' professional side.** Make a point of setting up "rules of engagement" and sticking to them so that you don't feel like you're getting taken advantage of in the situation. For instance, you can ask people to reschedule if they're more than 10 minutes late, or if you own a business, you can put in some type of consequences for last-minute canceled appointments.

  - **Spontaneous personal side.** If serious planners really stress you out in certain situations, such as going on an out-of-town trip, you can decide not to go with them or to plan in unstructured time where you can do as you please in the moment.

  - **Spontaneous professional side.** Commit to as few constraints as possible. For instance, instead of saying that you'll have something done by tomorrow, say that you'll have it done "soon." Or instead of giving a client a specific deadline by which you'll complete a project, tell the client that you'll give him or her weekly progress reports.

- **Step 4: Develop systems.** You can also establish simple routines t‍ help you to feel a greater sense of control and to avoid future frustrations and disappointments.
    - **Planners' personal side.** Before your significant other leaves the house each morning, remind him or her about what he or she needs to remember that day.
    - **Planners' professional side.** Make a note to send a follow-up reminder to more spontaneous coworkers a day or two before you're counting on them for something. It also rarely hurts to remind them the day of an event.
    - **Spontaneous personal side.** Set aside time during the week when you're completely free to do as you please, whether that means sleeping most of the day, going shopping, working late, or doing whatever else catches your fancy.
    - **Spontaneous professional side.** Try to negotiate to work from home at least one day per week so that you have more freedom in how, when, and where you get your work done.
- **Repeat steps 1 through 4 as needed.**

Love Someone

In the end, you will always encounter some differences between yourself and individuals of other personality types. Especially when it comes to those people with a permanent place in your life, such as family members, you can choose the way of frustration or that of love. In a commencement speech for the Nanyang Technological University in Singapore, Adrian Tan shared this priceless wisdom[3]:

> *I exhort you to love another human being. It may seem odd for me to tell you this. You may expect it to happen naturally, without deliberation. This is false. Modern society is anti-love. We've taken a microscope to everyone to bring out their flaws and shortcomings. It's far easier to find a reason not to love someone, than otherwise. Rejection requires only one reason. Love requires complete acceptance. It is hard work. . . . In loving someone, we become inspired to better ourselves in every way. . . . Loving is good for the soul.*

· ·

Journaling Exercise: Choosing Peace

Most of this book has focused on how you can experience peace for yourself, but this final chapter challenges you to seek peace with others. In closing, I would like you to take some time to reflect on how you can improve your relationships with those around you by answering the following questions.

Journaling Questions

- Did I see myself in Lucy or in Jason?

- Where do I regularly experience conflict relating to time personality issues?

- What can I do to improve the situation?

- How could I communicate with the other people involved?

- How can I choose peace regardless of the circumstances?

· ·

Notes

1. Stephen R. Covey, *The 7 Habits of Highly Effective People*. New York: Free Press, 2004.

2. Kerry Patterson, Joseph Grenny, Rob McMillan, and Al Switzler, *Crucial Conversations: Tools for Talking When Stakes Are High*. New York: McGraw-Hill, 2002.

3. Adrian Tan, "Don't Work. Be Hated. Love Someone," Half & Half. Available at: http://halfhalf.posterous.com/dont-work-be-hated-love-someone.

IN GRATITUDE

Mom and Dad, you have been the two biggest influences in my life, and I'm incredibly blessed to be your daughter. Thank you for always supporting me and believing in me and creating a nurturing family environment for me and my three awesome siblings to thrive.

Thank you also to all my teachers, coaches, peers, and mentors who have pushed me and challenged me to learn and grow. I appreciate each and every one of you, even though I'm only able to name a few. Mrs. Wheeler, Miss Robert, Mrs. Byrd, and Mrs. Fasolo, your teaching careers made an enormous positive impact on my life. All my amazing time coaching clients and training participants, it's an honor to collaborate with you on a daily basis. Thank you for being committed to the process of transformation. Cal Newport, Julia Knoll, Scott Barry Kaufman, Giles Anderson, Stephanie Frerich, and Abigail Saunders, thank you for playing an instrumental role in turning this book concept into a reality.

Many thanks also to my amazing friends who kept me encouraged during this process, particularly Lindsey, Jennifer, Lynne, Shay, Lisa, the Dahan family, and the Dayton ladies.

God—where would I be without you? Thank you for the gift of love, of hope, of faith, and of saving grace. I delight to do your will and to bring you glory.

BUT WHAT ABOUT . . . ?

Where to Find Answers to Your Questions

For fast-acting relief, try slowing down.

—LILY TOMLIN

- **What if I have a lack of desire and discipline to follow through?**
  - Skim through the "Red Flags" in Chapter 2 and "How to Pacify Your Inner Routine Rebel" in Chapter 6, and look at Chapter 8 for insight on building in accountability.
- **What if I've just gone through a major challenge, such as an illness?**
  - Go to the section on "Guilt" in Chapter 5 to learn how to reset others' expectations of you, and go through Chapter 7 to help you build routines that fit your current circumstances.
- **What if I'm in a seemingly impossible situation?**
  - Go to the section on "Balancing and Rebalancing" in Chapter 4 to determine if you face a major systemic decision, a situational strategy change, or a tough phase or season.
- **What if I'm feeling really drained because of time management conflicts?**
  - Go to Chapter 9 to discover how to reduce the drama and to recover quickly if it does happen.
- **What if I don't have time to implement everything in this book?**
  - Review the section on "Perfectionism" in Chapter 5, and then give yourself permission to start making changes in a less-than-ideal manner. Even initially clumsily executed change is better than no

improvement. The done-for-you routines in Chapter 7 can give you a jump-start.

- **What if I'm in a bad work environment?**
  - Review "Your Personal Definition of Success" and "Do You Thrive in Your Work Environment?" in Chapter 4 to determine whether it's time for a change.
- **What if I struggle with attention deficit disorder (ADD)/attention deficit hyperactivity disorder (ADHD)?**
  - Check out the resources under "Your Time Personality" in Chapter 1, and consider seeking out professional medical help.
- **What if I want more information on effective time investment?**
  - For exclusive time investment material, go to www.Schedule Makeover.com. You can also find more articles, resources, and information on coaching and training at www.RealLifeE.com.

Elizabeth Grace Saunders is an internationally recognized expert on achieving more success with less stress. She is the founder and CEO of Real Life E, a time coaching and training company that has helped clients on six continents to accomplish more with peace and confidence. Her methodologies empower individuals to move forward on their goals and companies to maximize the effectiveness of their workforce, including knowledge workers, sales staff, remote employees, and project managers. She also has spoken to thousands of individuals, including speaking after Steve Forbes at a business retreat.

Elizabeth has appeared as an expert in numerous offline and online media outlets, including *Forbes, Harvard Business Review, TIME, Mashable, London Evening Standard, Woman's Day, Inc., Design*Sponge, Huffington Post,* and NBC. *Stiletto Woman* named Elizabeth one of the "Top 25 Amazing Women of the Year."